HOW
CONGRESS
WORKS

HOW CONGRESS WORKS *and Why You Should Care*

Lee H. Hamilton

Indiana University Press

BLOOMINGTON AND INDIANAPOLIS

This book is a publication of
INDIANA UNIVERSITY PRESS
601 North Morton Street
Bloomington, IN 47404-3797 USA

http://iupress.indiana.edu

Telephone orders   800-842-6796
Fax orders   812-855-7931
Orders by e-mail   iuporder@indiana.edu

The paper used in this publication meets the minimum requirements of American National Standard for Information Sciences—Permanence of Paper for Printed Library Materials, ANSI Z39.48-1984.

MANUFACTURED IN THE UNITED STATES OF AMERICA

Library of Congress Cataloging-in-Publication Data

Hamilton, Lee.
  How Congress works and why you should care / Lee H. Hamilton.
      p. cm.
Includes index.
  ISBN 0-253-34425-5 (cloth : alk. paper) — ISBN 0-253-21695-8 (pbk. : alk. paper)
  1. United States. Congress. I. Title.
  JK1021H36 2004
  328.73—dc22

                                                    2003017926

1 2 3 4 5 09 08 07 06 05 04

Contents

Preface

One conclusion I drew from thousands of public meetings over thirty-four years with my southern Indiana constituents was that many people do not have a very complete understanding of the U.S. Congress—how it works, its role in American democracy, its impact on peoples' daily lives, and the ways that it can work better.

People were critical—frequently disappointed and rarely pleased with what Congress did. Mostly they were just puzzled by the institution that most directly represents their interests in our democracy.

In responding to their comments and questions, I often found myself spending as much time explaining and defending the institution of Congress as I did responding to specific inquiries. I tried to explain that Congress is the "First Branch" of the federal government, and that it is set up to be the most connected and responsive to the needs, desires, and aspirations of the American people. But Congress cannot function well if so many think that it is unresponsive or irrelevant. Our system of representative democracy is based upon people having both the right and responsibility to become involved in governance—skepticism of politicians and government is one thing, but giving up on this system entirely is another.

During my years as a Congressman, I tried to explain the work and role of Congress through these public meetings, discussions with constituents, and my weekly "Washington Report" newsletter. When I left public office and started the Center on Congress at Indiana University, my efforts expanded to include a wide variety of outreach methods, ranging from brief radio commentaries, to interactive, web-based "e-learning" modules for students.

One of my projects has been writing a monthly newspaper column that aims to explain to ordinary readers in plain language what Congress does, why Congress matters to people's daily lives, how Congress can improve, and why people should become more civically engaged. This book grew out of the various themes developed in more than fifty of these monthly columns, and my deep belief in the importance of educating the American people about the Congress and how they can participate in governance.

It simply would not have been possible to complete the book without the aid of Ken Nelson. Ken's keen eye, remarkable research and editorial skills, and deep and sympathetic view of the Congress helped shape the book through many drafts.

In addition to Ken, I received important assistance on the monthly columns from Rob Gurwitt and Phil Duncan.

Ted Carmines, Ben Rhodes, Don Wolfensberger, Ilona Nickles and Bob Huckfeldt provided valuable comments on the manuscript.

Janet Rabinowitch at Indiana University Press provided key guidance throughout the many months of putting the book together.

At a more fundamental level, I am indebted to my former colleagues in the Congress who helped me, listened to me, counseled me, and taught me my most important lessons about how Congress works.

Finally, I am particularly indebted to my family—my children Tracy, Debbie, and Doug, and most especially my wonderful wife Nancy—who recognized that my congressional duties would be demanding, but were unfailingly supportive nonetheless.

It is my sincere hope that these thoughts on Congress contribute in some small way to an improved public understanding of this fascinating, complex and essential institution of American democracy.

HOW
CONGRESS
WORKS

1

The Role of Congress

JAMES MADISON, principal drafter of the Constitution, held that in a representative democracy like ours, "the legislative authority necessarily predominates."[1] Take even a quick look at the powers given to Congress in the Constitution—passing the laws of the land, setting up and financing the departments of government, regulating commerce and trade, ratifying international treaties, raising and supporting our armed forces, declaring war—and it is very clear that our country's founders saw Congress as the foremost, dominant branch of our national government. They gave it most of the powers and had an impressive vision for what they clearly perceived as government's "First Branch."

On the other hand, many Americans today articulate a far less grand view of Congress, often not expressing much trust in it, rarely seeing it as a major factor in our nation's success. And a variety of sources—from administration officials to the media—will express or reinforce an executive-centered view of the government, with power drifting to the president, particularly when Congress doesn't live up to its responsibilities.

This chapter will try to sort this out—looking at the main roles and powers of Congress today, starting with why it really matters whether we have a Congress or not.

Why Congress Exists

I was once driving through southern Indiana on the way from one town meeting to another when I happened to turn on the radio. A commentator was attacking Congress. I don't remember exactly what we had done that annoyed him, but I do remember very clearly what he concluded. "We'd be a lot better off," he declared, "if we just did away with Congress!"

I remember thinking to myself how profoundly he misunderstood the U.S. Constitution and our system of representative democracy. "This fellow," I announced to the radio, "needs some lessons in American history."

You have to remember that the men who drew up our Constitution didn't want any single person to be able to impose his will on the country. They had just fought a war with England over that, and they didn't want to re-create anything like a monarchy on American soil. Just as important, they understood that even a leader who is elected by the people shouldn't be given too much power. That's why they divided the main powers of the federal government among the three branches. They believed freedom would be meaningless without a legislature independent of the president, able to represent the people of the United States in checking his desires.

Certainly the Congress has several important roles—to make the country work, to pass the budget, to manage conflict, to tackle the tough issues. Yet the most fundamental task of Congress is not to deal with any specific problem on the national agenda but to act as a check on the power of a single leader in order to maintain freedom for the American people. An independent legislature made up of representatives of the people is a key test of freedom in our country, or any country. Indeed, I doubt that freedom can exist—or ever has existed—in a nation without a free and independent parliament. So, ever since it was first set up as the First Branch in our system of government, the historic mission of Congress has been to maintain freedom.

If you visit the Capitol in Washington, look up as you approach the House of Representatives and you'll see, painted prominently above the entrance, Alexander Hamilton's statement, "Here, sir, the people govern." It is quite easy these days to proclaim cynically that Hamilton's words are just so much dust. Yet those who do are wrong, for Congress reflects us in all our strengths and all our weaknesses. It reflects our regional idiosyncrasies, our ethnic, religious, and racial diversity, our multitude of professions, and our shadings of opinion on everything from the value of war to the war over values. Congress is the government's most representative body. It is no accident that the founders gave it the power to make laws, to levy taxes, to decide how the government will spend its money, and to declare war. Congress gives the American people their voice in the counsels of power—or perhaps I should say "voices." By representing the multitude that we are, Congress is essentially charged with reconciling our many points of view on the great public policy issues of the day. That is why Congress often takes its time about things. To do their job, our representatives have to forge compromises, persuade others with the force of their arguments, and build a consensus behind an approach, if not a solution, to those issues.

I served in Congress long enough to know that it doesn't always do justice to all that the country's founders had in mind for it. But even when it doesn't serve a particular issue well, it still serves its larger purpose. "The numbers of men in all ages have preferred ease, slumber, and good cheer to liberty, when they have been in competition," John Adams wrote to his cousin, Samuel, in 1790. "We must not then depend alone upon the love of liberty in the soul of man for its preservation. Some political institutions must be prepared, to assist this love against its enemies."[2]

That is what Congress does—by acting as the people's voice against unchecked power, it is the guarantor of liberty. And for more than two hundred years, the American people have enjoyed a level of freedom only dreamt of in most other countries. That is why radio commentators who would wish it out of existence need to sit down, pick up an American history textbook, and think about it a little more.

Core Principle: Sovereignty of the People

Every summer, as the Fourth of July approaches, I'm struck by how inadequate a label "Independence Day" is. This certainly isn't to downplay the courage of our founders in declaring their independence from Great Britain or in fighting a war to guarantee it. But if you think about it, what we're really celebrating isn't a war; it's a concept. What was truly revolutionary about the American Revolution was the notion it enshrined that in a legitimate government, the people are sovereign, the ultimate rulers. Under this concept, neither Congress nor the president is supreme, because the ultimate authority lies with the people.

We take this idea for granted now, along with our system of representative democracy, because none of us has seen any other form of government in America, and because most other nations today—often following our example—are ruled by some sort of legislature chosen by the people. Yet at the time our system was being created, it was simply astonishing. To be sure, there were historical models dating to ancient Greece and Rome. But nothing was quite like what the framers devised, and certainly there were no models of such ambitious scope. The conventional wisdom of the day was that democracy on any but the smallest scale would quickly devolve into anarchy and mob rule.

"Again and again," historian Bernard Bailyn wrote about the founders, "they were warned of the folly of defying the received traditions, the sheer unlikelihood that they, obscure people on the outer borderlands of European civilization, knew better than the established authorities that ruled them; that they could successfully create something freer, ultimately more enduring than what was then known in the centers of metropolitan life."[3] The cry of "No taxation without representation" may have been born of frustration with dictates from the king of England, but it was rooted in the radical idea that people should have the final voice in their own governance.

The great phrases of the day ring through our history: "We the people," "consent of the governed," "blessings of liberty," "a more perfect union." These aren't just the technical terms of the scholars of political science. They are the words we live by, embodying the civic faith to which all Americans adhere. Our system rests squarely on the belief that freedom can only exist when one is governed with one's consent and with a voice in one's government. No one, the founders believed, is good enough to govern another person without his or her consent, and they embedded this concept in the bones of our system.

The question the framers had to grapple with, and one that remains a challenge for us today, was how to ensure that the people's views would be reflected in government. They recognized that a direct democracy—a system in which all citizens participate directly in making government decisions—had its limits. That might work for a small community whose citizens had the time and education to study their options before voting on how to proceed, but in a complex society it had severe drawbacks. Madison and his compatriots wanted to guard against the tyranny of the majority, to ensure that the passions of the moment could be cooled in deliberate debate, that the voice of the minority could be heard and its rights protected. And so they opted for a representative democracy, in which the people would choose elected representatives to carry their voices to Washington. This "representative assembly," John Adams wrote, "should be in miniature, an exact portrait of the people at large. It should think, feel, reason, and act like them."[4] Above all, it should be accountable to them.

This is, of course, the American experiment. No one knew whether dividing power among various branches and levels of government would ensure popular freedom and political ingenuity. No one knew whether, over the course of decades and then centuries, the two tyrannies feared by the founders—that of a strong executive, and that of a strong popular majority—could be constrained by a written constitution. And certainly no one knew whether Congress would, in fact, reflect the will of a teeming, diverse, and inventive society. At any given moment in our history, you could find Americans who would argue that the experiment was in danger of failing. Yet ours is now the oldest written constitution of a nation still in use, and its legitimacy remains solid. It has stood the test of time. But that does not guarantee it will stand all the tests of the future. We must never abandon our determination to make it a more perfect union.

Core Principle: Balancing Powers in Government

Some years ago I had the opportunity to spend several days in China with President Bill Clinton. At one of our stops, in a small community not far from Beijing, it fell upon me to explain the American system of government to a group of two or three hundred Chinese students. With only a few minutes to prepare, I did my best in the time I was allotted. The students were attentive and very polite, but I'm not sure I explained it as well as I should have. Indeed, I remember thinking to myself afterwards that I might have muffed a golden opportunity.

I have often thought about what I could have said to students from an entirely different culture to try to explain what the American system of government is all about. What is at the heart of our system that has allowed it to survive for so many years?

To me the key to understanding it is balance. The founders went to great lengths to balance institutions against each other—balancing powers among the three branches: Congress, the president, and the Supreme Court; between the House of Representatives and the Senate; between the federal government and the states; among states of different sizes and regions with different interests; between the powers of government and the rights of citizens, as spelled out in the Bill of Rights. The founders even discussed how the system they were creating could balance interest groups against one another.

The basic idea of balance is that no one part of government dominates the other. And it means that the decisions emerging from a process in which everyone has the right to participate are, in a sense, shared decisions, carrying with them a sense of authority and legitimacy.

Throughout the Constitution is an elaborate system of checks and balances to prevent abuse and concentration of power. Congress has the primary responsibility for passing the laws of the land, yet the president has the role of either signing them into law or vetoing them, and the courts can review whatever Congress passes. The president nominates judges to the Supreme Court, but the Senate must approve them. The president negotiates the treaties, but it is up to the Senate to ratify or reject them. The federal courts can declare laws passed by Congress and executive actions unconstitutional, yet it is Congress that creates and funds the federal courts, determines their jurisdiction, and has the power to remove judges. The president is in charge of the executive branch departments and agencies, yet Congress creates them, regularly monitors their activities, and provides their funding. And the list of shared responsibilities goes on.

The resulting system is a complicated maze of boxes and arrows on a flow chart that I would never expect my Chinese audience—or any other audience—to follow. But the underlying idea is a simple one: Our founders believed that the accumulation of power in any person or institution was dangerous and that balancing them off, one against the other, protected against tyranny. The challenge was to create a government that was powerful enough to act, but not with uncontrolled or unchecked power.

This balance of powers is one of the handful of core principles that has allowed our system of government to adapt to changing conditions over the past two hundred years. Rather than trying to devise a perfectly crafted, detailed system of government and setting it in stone, our founders provided the basic framework for our system of representative democracy with core principles like the balance of powers, the rule of law, majority rule (but with respect for minority rights), and making national laws "the supreme Law of the Land," under which there is flexibility for adjustment and change over the years. Thus, for example, the question of how the war-making power is balanced between the president and Congress is *still* being worked out, and in recent years the Supreme Court has rejected some Congress-passed methods of reviewing executive agency actions.

Yet the enduring principle that powers should be balanced in fundamental ways to ensure that no single part of government dominates and to protect against tyranny remains at the very heart of our system of government. This means that our system sometimes moves much more slowly than many of us might want. And it means that hearing from the many voices may sometimes lead to contentious debate. But to the founders, dispute and delay are simply part of the balanced system that prevents individuals or groups from imposing their will on the country.

The American people, despite their criticism of politics and politicians, have an unshakeable faith in the Constitution and in the American system of government and its power-sharing arrangements. The performance of government may disappoint them, but they firmly support the basic structure of our government set up by the founders. During all my years in Congress I never heard a constituent repudiating it. Americans believe that ours is the best system in the world and that it provides a framework for dealing with difficult policy issues while preserving our freedom. It may not be perfect or easy to explain, but it has served us well.

Key ways in which our system balances powers will be explored in the next two sections.

Congress and the President

Once a year, it's hard for Americans, ordinarily absorbed in their day-to-day activities, to avoid the news from Washington, as every television and radio network and every major newspaper covers the president's annual State of the Union address to a joint session of Congress.

On that night, all eyes are trained on the president as he outlines his priorities for the coming year. Members of the House and Senate from both parties applaud respectfully, sometimes enthusiastically. In this annual ritual of American democracy, the president tries to set a direction for the country, but in most speeches he also comes across as the nation's "chief legislator," giving the Congress its "to-do" list for the year.

It is important to remember, however, that the Constitution does not envision a master-and-servant relationship between the president and Congress. The framers of the document took care to create a system of government in which there is a balance of powers and extensive checks and balances between them. Indeed, the framers gave more specific powers to Congress, for they were wary that a too-powerful president would repeat the wrongs that the king of England had inflicted on the colonies. And they gave it a degree of independence from the executive that even today is rare among the world's major democracies.

One of my favorite remarks about the relationship between Congress and president came from former Speaker of the House Sam Rayburn. "I served with, not under, eight presidents," he often said. That probably sums up the sentiments of most members of Congress.

In our system, the president is entitled to propose legislation, but the Congress is equally entitled to dispose of it. His success at seeing his agenda enacted depends to a considerable degree on his skill at reaching out to legislators and persuading them to follow his lead. Because of the balance of powers, he cannot dictate to Congress what he wants, and he faces a huge task in communicating with

Congress because its very large number of members—535—hold many differing perspectives and represent diverse regional interests. The president often sees Congress as an obstacle to be overcome, and he always needs to calculate how his proposals will play out with Congress. One instrument of persuasion is the presidential veto, and sometimes with an overtly combative stance, a president can bend Congress to his will. But fostering a sense of cooperation and partnership with Congress—building coalitions of support—is typically the path to presidential success.

These days, we are accustomed to the notion of a president who is active across a broad front of legislative issues. But until the twentieth century, this was not the usual model of presidential behavior. Before then, more often than not, Congress was the driving force in American government.

In the nineteenth century, prominent congressmen such as Kentucky's Henry Clay were titans on the Washington stage for decades, while presidents came and went. For instance, when Indiana's William Henry Harrison was elected president in 1840, it was widely understood that he would look to Senator Clay for decisions on most important matters.

But in the first half of the twentieth century, presidents such as Theodore Roosevelt, Woodrow Wilson, and Franklin D. Roosevelt created the model of the expansive, activist modern presidency. To members of Congress, the president now looms large in the legislative process. He sets the national agenda and has behind him the vast knowledge and expertise of the federal bureaucracy. Using the "bully pulpit," the president can go over the heads of Congress and make his case directly to the American people. In this media-driven age, he speaks with one voice, rather than the 535 emanating from the halls of Congress, making it easier for him to command the attention of the cameras. The media seeks simplicity and vividness, and these are not qualities that Congress typically displays.

The relationship between Congress and the president is central to the workings of our system of government, and tension and struggle between these two rivals for power is inevitable under our Constitution. The framers did not set out to promote gridlock between them, but they did want to balance one off against the other and make sure that conflicting opinions in society should be considered carefully before government acts.

Ours is clearly not a system set up for quick, efficient action, and sorting out who has the real power between the president and Congress on a host of matters is not easy. But more often than not, Congresses and presidents find a way to work with each other, cooperating where possible, and the nation's business gets done. Their relationship, while at times tumultuous, in the end safeguards the people from corruption of power and abuse of authority—by either side. It is a system that works—not perfectly, to be sure, but certainly more than adequately.

Why Federalism Works

Early in my congressional career, I discovered a simple truth about our governmental system: It's confusing. Like most new members of Congress, I had taken office with visions of wrestling with the future of our Republic. So it came as something of a shock to learn that much of what my constituents wanted from me was help in navigating the federal, state, and local bureaucracies.

If you think back to your seventh-grade civics class, you'll remember learning about a system that resembles a layer cake, with local government at the bottom, the states in the middle, and the federal government at the top, all clearly delineated. That's still how most of us think of "federalism," or the division of responsibilities among different levels of government. But we're hopelessly out of date. If anything, the American political system is like a marble cake, with a blend of elected and appointed officials from all levels of government sharing policy and program duties.

Think about transportation, for instance. It's difficult enough to figure out which agency at which level of government maintains a particular stretch of roadway. But it can be next to impossible to untangle how a given decision was made about putting it there in the first place. The funding was provided by Congress, as were certain guidelines on how the money could be spent, but the specifics were up to a welter of state, county, and local elected officials and highway engineers. You can find the same assortment of responsibilities in everything from the administration of welfare benefits to law enforcement to cleaning up toxic waste.

There's a reason for this. As with many of the questions we sort through as a nation, the basic framework for dividing governmental responsibilities was set by the Constitution. Although the founders were quite specific on some matters—states, for instance, don't have the power to declare war or coin money—they deliberately left much room for flexibility. Just as they believed that dividing power among the various branches of the federal government would make it more responsive, so would dividing power among the different levels. "[It] is not by the consolidation, or concentration of powers, but by their distribution, that good government is effected," Thomas Jefferson wrote. "Were not this great country already divided into states, that division must be made, that each might do for itself what concerns itself directly, and what it can so much better do than a distant authority. . . . Were we directed from Washington when to sow, and when to reap, we should soon want bread."[5]

And so, over the decades, each level of government has seen its share of responsibilities ebb and flow with the demands of the era. The New Deal, for instance, brought new power to Washington, with its myriad of federal agencies helping American individuals and communities cope with the aftermath of the Depression; so, too, did the civil rights movement, which relied on federal authority to bring about change in the states. On the other hand, over the last two decades a mix of federal cutbacks, legislative changes, and Supreme Court decisions have returned authority to the states and even local communities. In some cases, this has been driven by an ideological belief that problems should be resolved closer to where people actually live, rather than by federal power. In other cases, it has been driven by practicality, as new approaches to problems bubble up from the states—as was the case with welfare reform.

We live in an era that is more difficult to categorize. On the one hand, the federal government has responded to the threat of terrorism by expanding and consolidating its power, especially for its various law enforcement and national security agencies. At the same time, however, the attorneys general in the various states have been responding to slow action at the federal level by taking on more responsibility for consumer enforcement in everything from policing Wall Street to suing drug makers for blocking lower-cost competitors. The distribution of power is constantly shifting, and sometimes, as at the moment, it moves in different directions simultaneously. In addition, the private sector today is often very much involved in carrying out government activities with government funding, so even the line between the government and the private sector is eroding.

For an ordinary citizen trying to get answers to a specific problem, this can be confusing and exasperating. This is why, when I was in Congress, my staff and I spent so much time directing constituents to the office and the level of government (or even private sector group) that could best help them. It can also lead to conflict within the system, as when states sue a federal agency they believe has failed to live up to its responsibilities. But rather than being a fundamental design flaw, the flexibility created by our Constitution allows for a pragmatic response to the evolving challenges we face as a nation. It creates the chance for policymakers to gauge whether problems are best confronted in town halls or state capitals or Washington—or in some combination of all of them—and then to work together to assign each level of government its appropriate role. That these roles change over time is a sign not of weakness but of the system's enduring strength.

Key Power:
Passing the Basic Laws of the Land

When a country is being organized, one of the most basic decisions is who makes the laws. The lawmaking body could be the king, the party secretary, the supreme council, or the militia, but in our system of government, it's the Congress. The very first thing our Constitution does is to grant Congress the core power of making the basic laws of the land, declaring in Article 1, Section 1 that "All legislative powers herein granted shall be vested in a Congress of the United States."

Certainly the president plays a very important role in the process, setting his agenda for the nation, recommending bills to Congress, threatening to veto legislation he opposes. But the main lawmaking responsibility rests with Congress, and its powers under the Constitution are awesome. Formally, it has the power to wipe out with a single law the entire executive branch, except for the president and vice president, and to abolish all federal courts, except for the Supreme Court, which it could reduce to a single judge with minor jurisdiction.[6] Many of Congress's legislative powers are specifically listed in the Constitution; others are implied. Over the years the courts have interpreted Congress's powers in such sweeping terms that it can legislate in almost every aspect of American life.

Lawmaking can be a complicated and intimidating process; one congressional report listed more than one hundred specific steps a bill might go through in the process of becoming a law.[7] But at its core—as I would often point out in my high school assembly speeches—it simply means trying to understand the hopes, needs, dreams, and desires of the American people and translating that into public policy through the legislative process. The American people tell members of Congress to do or not to do certain things, and they express basic interests and values. It is these experiences which are the basis of lawmaking.

But lawmaking is not done in a vacuum. It is carried out in an intensely partisan atmosphere, with one party competing against another, in very hard-fought battles. People feel deeply on both sides of the issue, and a lot is at stake—huge amounts of money, special programs, new benefits. In the legislative process, worthy groups compete for limited resources: younger people want more for education, for example, while older people want more for Social Security and Medicare. The place where we work out worthy, though conflicting, goals on the national level is Congress. The process produces winners and losers and can generate hard feelings, often lingering for some time, which is why a skillful legislator always tries to minimize the impact on the losing side.

The legislative process can be drawn out, untidy, and contentious, because Congress is trying to make the laws for a very large, highly diverse country. The complexity of the process reflects the complexity of the country. In a democratic society, the role of government is to moderate the tension among competing interests and to make it easier for people to strive toward the kind of life they want to lead. It is not easy, but it is essential that the tensions and the strife within a country of 300 million people be harmonized and accommodated. Congress's process of extensive deliberation, negotiation, and compromise often works, but not always. The great blot in our nation's history, the Civil War, showed all too painfully what can happen when social conflict cannot be resolved through the normal congressional process.

Ever since its first major bill—the Tariff Act of 1789, which imposed duties on imported goods in order to finance the new government's functions—Congress has approved more than 50,000 bills on every conceivable topic. In my very first Congress, I cast votes to pass the landmark Voting Rights Act of 1965, to set up Medicare and Medicaid, to approve the first general federal aid to elementary and secondary schools, to approve the student aid program for undergraduates, to set up two new cabinet-level departments (HUD and Transportation), and to pass and send to the states the Twenty-fifth Amendment to the Constitution on presidential succession, among many others. Legislators never cease to be amazed by the incredible variety of issues coming before them.

Giving this core lawmaking power to Congress was a major experiment by the framers, but it has generally served the nation well. As will be explored further in chapter 3, the process through which Congress reconciles competing views and makes the basic laws of the land is dynamic, complex, and untidy. Yet in the end I believe it is reasonably—not perfectly—responsive to the expressed desires of the American people. And it has generally—not always—allowed our nation to work through our differences peaceably for more than two hundred years. Above all, it is an ongoing process, for in a democratic society no issue is ever settled once and for all but is revisited again and again.

Key Power: Controlling the Purse

Ask the average American what Congress accomplishes, and the answer usually comes back: not much. Progress in Washington can be slow, with strong differences of opinion among legislators reflecting the fact that they deal with a large number of exceedingly difficult problems and come to the nation's capital representing all corners of our nation. Some issues on the agenda—like abortion—keep coming back for years, even decades, and never seem to be resolved. Yet on one of its most important responsibilities, Congress year after year is able to overcome differences and in the end reach an agreement that helps set national priorities.

That responsibility is Congress's "power of the purse"—its ability to set the spending and taxing policies of the nation. Not one dime can be spent from the federal treasury without the approval of Congress. The determination of the budget is usually the most important political process in Congress any given year, partly because of its size (more than $2 trillion) and partly because it is the principal means by which government establishes its priorities.

The framers of the Constitution, mindful of "taxation without representation" suffered by colonists under the British, took care to specify in the Constitution that the ultimate power to tax and spend resides in the hands of the legislative branch—which is closer to the people—not the executive branch. And it is without doubt one of Congress's most important powers. In the *Federalist,* James Madison called it "the most complete and effectual weapon with which any constitution can arm the immediate representatives of the people."[8] It checks the power of the president and gives Congress vast influence over American society, because federal spending reaches into the life of every citizen.

The annual consideration of the federal budget is an enormously complex undertaking—even more difficult to explain than the process through which a bill becomes law—and it can be highly contentious. The budget submitted to Congress by the president is often proclaimed "dead on arrival" by the opposition party; headlines throughout the year declare that the president and congressional leaders "clash on spending," and competing factions warn that if they don't get their way, a budgetary "train wreck" will occur and the government will shut down.

That rarely happens, and even if it does, the deadlock doesn't last for long. To be sure, the movement toward compromise may sometimes be slow and tortured. But in the end, the House and Senate reach an accommodation with each other, and with the president, that enables the federal government to meet its responsibilities from programs as large as Social Security and national defense to activities as small as repairing the panda cages at the National Zoo.

I don't want to overstate what Congress does. The vast majority of the spending items in the president's budget submission to Congress are approved every year. Congress will debate his budget and make various revisions, but most years the president largely gets what he wants. In many respects he is the chief budget maker, and Congress is the chief budget approver. The work involved in doing this is arduous, and—a reflection of its importance—it is the single most time-consuming thing Congress does. One veteran observer of Congress, asked to estimate how much time members spend on budgetary matters, replied: "Almost all." That's an exaggeration, but it may not seem like it during those many weeks each year when Congress is preoccupied with the budget resolution or the appropriations bills—sorting through thousands of recommendations, holding hundreds of hearings, casting hundreds of votes. In recent decades, about half of all House roll call votes have been budget related; in the Senate the percentage is even higher.

The multilayered congressional budget process has its shortcomings. And it is so complex and unwieldy that it is difficult for legislators, let alone the public, to follow. Constituents, who would often be confused by the work of Congress, would be overwhelmed by the complexities of the budget process, as well as by the amounts of money involved. Billions of dollars are so outside their experience that their eyes glaze over as politicians start talking about budget figures. As one constituent said to me in exasperation, "What difference does it make—a few million or a few billion?"

The average American may not know all about the several thousand pages of the federal budget, yet in the end Americans do know that Congress perseveres and ultimately fulfills the major responsibility assigned it in Article 1, Section 8 of the Constitution—"to pay the Debts and provide for the common Defence and general Welfare of the United States."

Key Power: Shaping Foreign Policy

Once, when Harry Truman was president, someone asked him who made U.S. foreign policy. His reply was simple: "I do."

No president today could make that claim. Indeed, not since John F. Kennedy was president has foreign policy been the preserve of even a few policy makers, let alone just one. As our country engages the world with renewed vigor and interest after the September 11 attacks, this is worth keeping in mind. Congress, too, is an important player in foreign affairs, a fact that might seem inconvenient in a time of crisis but that actually benefits the country in many ways. It is worth remembering that in terms of foreign policy powers specifically enumerated in the Constitution, Congress was granted more than the president.

Presidents have never been particularly keen about this splitting of foreign policy powers between the legislative and executive branches. Early on, President Jefferson stated, "The transaction of business with foreign nations is executive altogether." A Reagan administration official put this sentiment more graphically: "Involving Congress in foreign affairs is like having 535 ants sitting on a log floating down a turbulent river—each one thinking he is steering."[9]

There is no doubt that the president is the chief foreign policy maker. His control over the executive branch and command of the national stage give him enormous power to influence the foreign policy debate and to rally public and international support behind a particular cause. And in recent years Congress has devolved considerable power to the president to declare and wage war. Yet he regularly works within the framework of policies that exist in the laws passed by Congress. When Congress and the president understand their respective roles in foreign policy and make an effort to work together, better policy emerges.

True, it can be difficult for a president to work with Congress. For one thing, senators and representatives as a whole tend to focus more on domestic issues, just as their constituents do, and many give limited thought to foreign affairs except when a vote is pending or a crisis breaks. It is also true that power on Capitol Hill is diffuse, and it shifts with each issue. In the old days, the president could consult with Congress simply by talking to a few important congressional leaders and committee chairmen. Today, dozens of members of Congress and many congressional committees play major roles in foreign policy. Members are younger, more aggressive, better informed, more diverse, and less respectful of traditional authority. It no longer works for the president to consult with a handful of people and assume that the rest of Congress will go along.

We should also remember that the writers of our Constitution never envisioned an entirely unfettered presidency in foreign affairs. The president may be commander in chief, but the Constitution gave Congress the power to declare war, make the nation's laws, and pay for whatever policies the president pursues. The president has the power to negotiate treaties, but they cannot take effect unless the Senate ratifies them—and, in many cases, unless both the House and Senate pass laws to implement them. Without cooperation, in other words, some of the most basic tools of foreign policy cannot be used successfully.

And the plain truth is, no wise chief executive would want to try. American foreign policy always has more force and punch to it when the president and Congress speak with one voice. As the most representative branch of government, Congress best articulates the concerns of different segments of the population. When the president takes these views into consideration in formulating foreign policy, the policy that results is more likely to have strong public support.

During my years in Congress, I probably devoted more time to foreign affairs than any other single area. As a freshman member from rural southern Indiana, I wanted to serve on a House committee dealing with domestic matters, but for some reason never quite made clear to me, I was assigned to the House Foreign Affairs Committee. I stuck with it because I came to appreciate the important role Congress could play in shaping a sound foreign policy for the nation, both as an informed critic and as a constructive partner.

Yet throughout those years I was disappointed in every administration's consultation with Congress on major foreign policy issues. Often the administration contacted just a few select legislators, failed to consult on a regular, sustained basis, and frequently approached Congress after a decision had been made rather than seeking genuine input. Prominent examples of poor consultation were the Vietnam War of the sixties and seventies, and the Contra War in Nicaragua during the eighties. In both cases, policy was controlled by a small group of high-level officials, and few others either inside or outside the executive branch knew the full extent of our government's activities. It would be hard to argue that the country was well served by this approach.

Although it may seem awkward to have to consult with congressional leaders, presidents can profit from the experience. The president can be quite isolated in our system of government. As Lyndon Johnson's press secretary, George Reedy, once put it, in the White House no one tells the president to go soak his head. But members of Congress do not serve at the pleasure of the president, and that independence gives their advice added weight. The president may not like or take their advice, but he will probably forge better policy if he considers it.

On the tough foreign policy questions, the president needs help; the decisions should not be made by just one person. The framers wisely sought to encourage a creative tension between the president and Congress that would produce policies that both advance national interests and reflect the views of the American people.

Congress and Individual Liberties

Congress has clearly been given an extensive range of powers; some would say too many. One of my constituents would always comment how glad he was to see me back in Indiana, because then he knew Congress was not in session and was unable, as he put it, to "do any mischief."

A perennial constituent complaint is that Congress has too much power to interfere with personal freedoms. The perception is of a massively powerful institution that disrupts and invades our lives and undermines our individual liberties.

This is one of the most durable issues in American public life. Since the nation was founded, Americans have debated the proper balance between the rights of individuals to live their own lives and the power of Congress and the president to govern the country and make it secure. My guess is that we will continue to debate this question for as long as we endure.

That is because the founders themselves were unsettled on the matter. They wanted Congress to have extensive powers. But they were wary of granting it unfettered authority, particularly the ability to infringe too greatly on individual liberty. As Richard Henry Lee, one of the Virginia signers of the Declaration of Independence, wrote in 1787, as the nation was debating whether it needed an explicit Bill of Rights, "[T]he most express declarations and reservations are necessary to protect the just rights and liberty of Mankind from the silent powerful and ever active conspiracy of those who govern."[10]

Even the Bill of Rights, though, leaves a lot of room for interpretation. Ever since it was enacted we've gone back and forth on how far Congress and the president can go in abridging personal freedom, from the Alien and Sedition Acts over two hundred years ago, to our ongoing debates over gun control and abortion rights, to the more recent questions being raised over how far civil liberties can be trimmed in order to fight terrorism. The extent of Congress's power when it comes to individual rights is no cut-and-dried issue with easy answers. You could argue that debating it is fundamental to our character, a part of our genetic makeup as a nation.

This is true even though Congress's power is limited in ways that go well beyond the Bill of Rights. To begin with, the founders placed explicit restrictions within the body of the Constitution itself. Congress cannot pass *ex post facto* laws, for instance, or pass any bills of attainder—that is, legislation that declares someone guilty of an offense without trial. They also resorted to the core strategy of balancing power among Congress, the president, and the judiciary, making congressional action subject both to the president's veto and to the Supreme Court's rejection.

Congress is also hemmed in by political reality. It is a large body, with two separate institutions—the House and the Senate—each with its own traditions and temperament. They do not, by nature, see eye to eye, and each has its own crowded agenda of complex issues. Even within one chamber, finding common ground among all the various factions, regional interests, and ideologies can be quite difficult. People often complain about congressional inefficiency, but it is part of what safeguards our rights as citizens. Then too, forces outside Congress, from lobbyists and political parties to the overall judgment of the American people, constrain its actions. Simply put, once most Americans arrive at a firm opinion about a matter of public policy, particularly regarding their individual liberties, Congress will be hard-pressed to ignore it. Congress may be the most powerful legislative body in the world, but I can tell you from personal experience that anyone who serves in it also gets a keen sense of the limitations on its power.

This is a particularly tricky question when, as recently, there have been voices in the country at large pressing Congress to weigh in on the administration's efforts to prevent terrorist acts by broadening federal wiretap authority and expanding domestic spying capabilities. Others counter that Congress's role is simply to go along, but of course that's not so. It is one of the American system's marks of genius that we always have one branch keeping an eye on the other, and one of Congress's roles is to act on behalf of the American people as the guardian of our guardians: slowing things down when needed, requiring that fewer decisions be made in secret, guarding against unchecked powers. As Justice Louis Brandeis rightly observed, the American people "must look to representative assemblies for the protection of their liberties."[11] The founders may have wanted to ensure that Congress did not wield too much power, but they also did not want it to wield too little, which is why oversight of the executive branch is fully as important a congressional role as writing new tax law or appropriating money for new programs.

Whatever the challenge to individual liberties today from whatever source, members of Congress have to grapple with what's right for the country at the moment, just as we debated the Bill of Rights, just as we've argued over other civil liberties through the centuries. Woodrow Wilson once said, "The country is always aborning," and in this ongoing American experiment, the question of how far the federal government can go in impinging on individuals' lives is never resolved but must be taken up by each generation anew.

The Roots of Our Success

Almost any way you look at it, we have been a remarkably successful country. The twentieth century was clearly the American century. I don't want to join those who elevate the United States to near-holy status; we're certainly not perfect. At various times our nation's standing ebbs and flows, and we only do so-so when compared with other industrialized countries on basic social measures such as infant mortality or income inequality. But overall it seems fair to say that in the broad ways societies are measured—economically, militarily, the extent of our cultural influence, the freedoms we offer our residents, the opportunities we present for individual success—the United States has flourished over the past few decades.

Ask anyone why this is and you'll get a long list of explanations: the dynamism of our private sector; the sheer breadth and vast natural resources of this country; the creativity, vitality, and independence of the American people; the liberties enshrined in the Bill of Rights. Yet there's another important contributor to our success that I'll warrant would not come up often in conversation, at least not in this day and age: our government. In a recent survey, fewer than one in ten people saw Congress as very responsible for the successes the country has experienced in the past century.

This is not to suggest that people think Congress and the president are simply bystanders in securing the country's fortunes. It's just that after years of antigovernment rhetoric, deepening partisanship, widening special-interest influence, and saturation press coverage of political conflicts and personal scandals, our government and our system of representative democracy tend not to rank high on Americans' lists of why our country has been flourishing. This is too bad, because they belong near the top. The citizens of a country cannot have well-being without good governance. While market economies are important and the private sector is important, they cannot function without a framework, determined by government, and that framework is provided by representative democracy.

In essence, our form of government is our answer to the extraordinarily difficult question of how best to organize a society. Countries, city-states, and empires have wrestled with this issue over the course of history, and some have tried what amounted to disastrous experiments. Our system has succeeded in large measure because over the long term it has both promoted the dynamic forces within our society and provided a means of keeping them in balance. From its very beginning, our nation's government has been involved in defining the rights and liberties individuals could exercise, laying the groundwork for developing the country's resources, setting up the structure within which businesses could operate freely and fairly, and providing the security—military, judicial, and social—necessary for people to pursue their ambitions and take advantage of the opportunities afforded them.

We rely on our government, through our elected representatives, to sort out these difficult issues as well as to help us lengthen our vision for the future. As former senator Robert Wagner put it, "If a government or a people is to progress, its goal must ever be a little beyond its reach."[12] It did not have to be that way. Our country would be vastly different if the framers had placed power in the hands of a single ruler or given much less voice to the American people. As it is, though, the greatest secret to our success may not be that we get the balance among competing forces right all the time. Rather, it's that we have, in Congress, the presidency, and the judiciary, a forum for deliberation in which every American can have a voice in the process and a stake in the product. This ability to work together to resolve our differences and set the basic framework for the country is what helps our nation to flourish and allows us to live together so peacefully, productively, and successfully.

Even though Americans will often complain about government and not see it as much of a factor in our nation's success, it's where they turn when the big problems arise—war, disaster, terrorism, recession, disease—or when their local bridge decays or their retirement is threatened. The various ways the work of Congress has affected people's everyday lives is explored in the next chapter.

2

The Impact of Congress

WHEN I WAS IN CONGRESS, I would often start off my local public meetings by asking whether anyone could name a federal program that worked well. Usually not a single hand went up—even when the audience was filled with people who received Social Security checks every month, who drove to the meeting on the interstate highway, or who had attended the local university with the help of federal student loans. The response of my constituents was fairly typical. In a recent poll, when people were asked what they thought was Congress's most important accomplishment that year, more than three-fourths responded: "Don't know."

I recognize that it is commonplace to dismiss Congress as largely irrelevant or a bumbling institution that cannot do anything right. Yet people who have served in it typically come away with a different view. Claude Pepper, whose service in Congress representing the state of Florida spanned six decades, once remarked: "The government of the United States belongs to the people of this land and whenever their troubles and their disasters and their needs impel its use, it is available. It is the mightiest institution on the face of the Earth, and it can be a hand that will lift up the people if they call upon it."[1]

This chapter will explore this question of how much of an impact the work of Congress has on people's lives today.

Congress and the Fabric of Our Lives

Like many Americans, I watched the electrifying march of the U.S. women's soccer team to victory in the 1999 World Cup with a mixture of awe and pride. I was taken, of course, by the athleticism and skill shown by our players, but I was equally delighted by something most Americans probably didn't recognize: the role that Congress had played in what I was watching.

It has been more than thirty years since we passed the measure known as Title IX. I was still a relatively junior member of the House when we voted on the bill, and although the rhetoric on the floor was high-minded and full-blown, as it tends to be at such moments, I'm not sure anyone fully grasped the depth of the changes we were enacting. It takes nothing away from the extraordinary accomplishments of the women on the soccer field to say that they and those who celebrate their accomplishments could thank Congress, in part, for the path that led them there.

"Title IX" refers to a law passed in 1972, a set of education amendments to the Civil Rights Act of 1964. It requires that women be given an equal opportunity to participate in all programs run by colleges and schools that receive federal funds. One of its results, the full measure of which we are just beginning to enjoy, is the explosion of women's sports. In the wake of the U.S. soccer players' victory, President Clinton referred to them as "Daughters of Title IX," and he was right.

It has been popular of late to view Congress as full of people who love the limelight and look out for themselves but who contribute little to the national well-being. Not long before I left Congress, for example, a group of constituents visiting my Indiana office told me exactly that: Congress has nothing to do with our daily lives, they informed me, except when it wants to tax or regulate us. As it happened, I knew these people fairly well, so I responded by asking them a few questions—about the interstate highway they took to my office, the once-polluted river they crossed over, and the bank or grocery store or pharmacy they were going to next. They soon saw where I was headed. Their lives had been profoundly affected by Congress. If you know how to look, I suggested, you can see Congress's contributions all around you.

Just what those contributions ought to be, of course, is the subject of serious debate, and rightly so. Americans have this conversation all the time, in Washington and at political gatherings around the country, and it is how we remain on course as a nation.

But too often of late we've gone beyond that, to thinking of Congress as an irrelevant institution with little or no connection to our everyday lives. So as you hear about the work of Congress on all the issues facing it—tax cuts, national security, the federal budget, health care—think about how they might affect your life personally instead of dismissing the debates as esoteric and meaningless. What if Congress cuts federal funding for basic research into high technology and other sciences? Will it just be trimming unneeded fat from the budget, or will it be doing away with work that could undergird our growth in the twenty-first century—and possibly, a few years down the road, provide you or someone in your family with a job? Or think about health care: Should Congress continue to help researchers who are looking for a way to cure AIDS or breast cancer or any of the other diseases that cause us to suffer? Or education: Should Congress find ways of helping parents choose the best school for their children, even if it means using public funds to allow children to attend parochial schools? These are hardly questions that are irrelevant to our daily lives.

But this is what Congress does. When it takes up issues like the education of our children, or the quality of the water we drink, or our ability to care for our parents as they age—or whether women should be treated equally by college programs—it is doing its best to reflect and to improve the quality of our lives as individuals and the strength of our nation. So as the budget and other issues come up for debate in Washington, and those of us who pay attention to such things start discussing them with our friends and neighbors in community halls and meeting places, we should be careful about falling into the trap of believing that nothing is at stake.

Government's Greatest Endeavors

Skepticism toward government has always been a healthy strain in American thinking. The Constitution, with its emphasis on dividing government as a way of checking official power, is one reflection of that view. In recent decades, we have seen the relative optimism about government of the early 1960s give way to a broader pessimism, with many believing that government creates more problems than it solves.

Government is certainly not perfect. There are inefficiencies, mistakes, and blunders. We should not overlook these, but neither should they form the overwhelming impression of what government does. A recent study on government's greatest achievements over the past half century reminds us that there is another side to the story.[2]

The study developed a list of more than five hundred major laws passed by Congress in the past fifty years and then surveyed hundreds of college professors, asking them to rank the greatest achievements. The national problems and challenges that spawned these laws were as complex and difficult as the legislative solutions themselves. High on the list of accomplishments were rebuilding Europe after World War II through the Marshall Plan; containing communism and winning the cold war; maintaining the world's greatest defense system; expanding equal access and the right to vote; reducing the incidence of deadly or crippling diseases; increasing the stability of financial institutions and markets; improving air and water quality; protecting wilderness; providing financial security in retirement through Social Security and Medicare; expanding foreign markets for U.S. goods; promoting space exploration; and increasing arms control and disarmament.

As I look through this list, what strikes me is how our lives are better and safer in many ways because of government activity. Granted, an equally interesting study could be done on government's greatest failures over the past half century. Yet the report is still a helpful and all too infrequent reminder that as a nation we have come far in seeking to end difficult and deep-seated problems both here and abroad. And that's the key point. America rightly emphasizes individual values and independence, but when epidemic disease threatens our health, when dangers lurk at our borders, when energy shortages develop, when foreign trade barriers harm our exports, or when business irregularities undermine investor confidence, part of the way to cope with these problems more effectively is through action in Congress.

Certainly not every action by legislators is a blockbuster. Paul Douglas, the distinguished senator from Illinois, once commented that when he was elected to the Senate he came with the idea of saving the world. After a few years, he decided he would be content with saving the United States. After ten years in office he hoped he could save Illinois, and when he was leaving office he said he would settle for saving the Indiana Dunes.

The truth is, progress is usually made inch by inch. Issues often need to be revisited more than once, and setbacks are at least as common as triumphs. Yet as America faces a host of challenges in the twenty-first century, we need a broader public recognition that while government may be part of the problem, it is also part of the solution.

An Ordinary Day

From time to time, some major event comes along to remind us of how much we actually depend on the U.S. government. So it was that, after the Oklahoma City bombing and again after the

September 11 attacks, public support for Congress and the federal government rose to its highest levels in years.

I'm always encouraged to see this support, but to my mind it misses a crucial point. Congress and the president aren't just there on those days of crisis that are forever etched in our memory, nor do big-ticket items such as the military or homeland defense tell the whole story of government's impact on Americans' lives. Rather, working with the president, Congress has found many important ways to improve the quality of the average person's life. Imagine an ordinary day, and I think you'll be astounded at how much you can take for granted that your parents and grandparents could not.

Let's start the moment you wake up in the morning. The radio/alarm clock that just went off? If you live in a rural area—or in a suburb that twenty years ago was farmland—you might give a thought to the 1936 Rural Electrification Act, which brought electricity to rural areas and promoted the development you've been able to enjoy. If you live in a city, congressionally mandated subsidies and regulations have played no small part in bringing that power to your electric outlets at a price you can afford.

Now that you're up and brushing your teeth, it wouldn't hurt to remember the 1974 Safe Drinking Water Act, which put the government in the business of setting standards for drinking-water quality and making sure they're met. We take the safety of the water that comes out of our taps for granted, but before that law's passage, potential cancer-causing chemicals were showing up in cities' water, lead from supply pipes was becoming a problem, and viral and bacteriological contamination of water in smaller communities had been growing. While you're standing in front of the mirror, it's also worth remembering that a great deal of what we've learned about curing disease and remaining healthy has come from research funded by Congress. Moreover, if you wear cosmetics, take vitamins, or use medications, they have had to run a gauntlet of safety tests because at some point in the past, horror stories about their lack of safety led Congress to react. So, too, when you sit down at the breakfast table, you're benefiting from meat and egg inspections carried out by the Department of Agriculture and agricultural programs run by the federal extension service in every county.

Now let's say that, like most commuters in the country, you drive to work. Almost every safety feature of the car you drive, from the seat belts to the air bags to the quality of the tires, has been strengthened either by congressional mandate or by the activities of the National Transportation Safety Board. Your car's fuel efficiency has grown because of congressional pressure on auto manufacturers, as has the quality of the air you breathe. Many of the roads you drive on, of course, were funded by Congress. And if you're riding mass transit, federal subsidies played a big role in allowing the system to exist in the first place, and federal laws regulate its safety.

Once you get to work, it's hard to turn around without encountering some way in which the federal government has improved your lot in life. From improving workplace safety to prohibiting job discrimination, protecting your pension, or providing federal support for the industry you work in or the industries your job depends on, your working life has been shaped by congressional action. This is just as true of your education before you began working. Your high school likely enjoyed federal support for everything from its library to its lunch program; the land grant college system was established by Congress, while other colleges and universities depend heavily on federal research grants; and your college tuition may well have been supported by a Pell grant or some other federal subsidy, as today some three-fourths of all student financial aid in the country is financed by the federal government.

Finally, let's take a moment to think about all the things you do outside of work or home. If you enjoy parks, or like to boat on unpolluted rivers, or use community centers, or go online in the evening, or write checks from your local bank, or have some portion of your investments in stocks, or buy your children toys, or depend on food labeling to help you decide how to feed your family, you owe a moment's thanks to Congress for the funding or the regulations or the organizations that make it possible.

To be sure, there will always be room for argument about how the federal government goes about these various responsibilities. Certainly the government doesn't always get it right or do it in the most efficient manner. People can legitimately disagree about whether this federal agency has gone too far in regulating the workplace or that one has not gone far enough in protecting the environment. But the impulse that lies behind federal action—the desire to produce a higher quality of life for all Americans—is much harder to argue with. There are issues of reliability, safety, and comfort you don't even notice today, because at some point in the past, someone in Congress took note and did something about them.

Congress Does More Work than Meets the Eye

Make a joke about politicians bickering in Washington and a "do-nothing Congress," and audiences will always chuckle and nod in agreement. This criticism is as old as the republic, and it is one that resonates. Harry Truman's 1948 denunciation of the "do-nothing Congress" was the campaign slogan that fueled his come-from-behind victory over Thomas Dewey. Newspapers have been eager to reinforce the theme, with headlines like "The Do-Nothing Congress? It's a Good Thing" and "Here's to a Do-Nothing Congress." Lately it seems that Americans' historic skepticism toward Congress has evolved into something more sinister—sheer cynicism.

It is true that sometimes Congress doesn't have a stunning record of accomplishment. It usually has a long list of unfinished business. Members themselves are acutely aware of this. Many times throughout the year—during weekends at home or holiday recesses—they appear before constituents and are asked simply: "What have you people in Congress accomplished?" Even leadership-supplied lists of talking points may not give legislators much help in coming up with anything close to a convincing response.

So I think it's important to point out two things about Congress. First, it is capable of passing legislation with sweeping impact on the lives of Americans, particularly if there is a clear national consensus behind an idea or if action is imperative due to an external crisis. And second, even when Congress is not producing blockbuster bills, members are typically working on scores of other, less-publicized matters that sustain and improve the quality of life here and abroad.

It's remarkable how quickly we forget that Congress has been involved in some big things in the last few years—from overhauling the welfare system and rewriting telecommunications laws to liberalizing trade laws and expanding NATO. If the current Congress passes few landmark bills, is it fair to say that members have failed to earn their pay? No. Some of their work involves laying the groundwork for future action on very complex matters that may take more than one Congress to resolve. The Clean Air Act and Immigration Reform Act, for instance, took multiple Congresses to complete due to their inherent complexity.

At other times, Congress is grappling with issues on which the citizens of the United States as well as the political parties strongly disagree, and achieving compromise is difficult. For most recent Congresses, voters stacked the deck against decisive legislative action by choosing a Congress led by one party and a White House occupied by the other. Congress's critics say "politics" is to blame for the deadlock, but look at it another way: Parties in a divided government are laying out their arguments on issues to voters, asking them to deliver a verdict at the polls in November that could help resolve the impasse. That's democracy in action. This process may be slow and frustrating, but democracy is like that sometimes—actually, much of the time. It's a tough job trying to make public policy for our nation, especially in the absence of clear and decisive signals from the voters.

Reporters tend to make premature judgments midstream about "do-nothing" Congresses and then cover the high-profile issues that provoke legislative conflict. The inclination of the media is to show what's wrong rather than what's right. Far less attention is given to the routine but vital work that Congress does in other matters, most notably the annual appropriations process, which funds the wide range of federal functions that touch the lives of every American. Every session of Congress passes legislation to fund the departments, agencies, and programs of the federal government, based on scrutiny of past performance. Moreover, dozens of bills are enacted that are bipartisan and noncontroversial in nature, and even though many may be more modest in scope, they still address specific problems and needs. And each year, Congress holds hearings to air major differences of opinion, oversees executive branch conduct, reviews treaties and presidential nominations, and addresses constituent problems.

Some Congresses certainly may seem less productive than others. Yet it is still unusual for the legislative output in any Congress to fall much below four hundred new bills passed and signed into law, and rarely does Congress adjourn without enacting at least a handful of major new laws over its two-year cycle. Members, after all, recognize that they are legislators and their responsibility is to produce. Even when a Congress doesn't earn a big place in the history books, more is going on in the Congress than is often recognized.

A Balanced View of Congress

When I was in Congress, a curious thing would happen several times a year. A group of financial professionals would visit my office, sit down with me, and ask for some small change to the laws affecting them. What was strange about this was not that they were lobbying me—lots of people did that—but how they did so. Most groups, when they get a chance to meet a member of Congress, are curious about lots of things, especially the big issues: the economy, the deficit, foreign affairs. This group, though, only wanted to talk about the one seemingly minor change affecting their profession, with very technical legislation and very specific language in mind. Once that was done, they would go on to the next congressional office.

Now, they were doing nothing improper. But their lack of interest in the bigger picture struck me. When professional groups focus narrowly on their own interests, it's usually a sign that Congress needs to weigh their proposals carefully and look at the broader national interest. Sometimes, though, Congress fails to do this. When that happens, the results can be painful: Witness the recent corporate scandals coming after Congress's indulgent treatment of the financial and accounting communities.

This is worth remembering, because it hints at a reason why Congress can make mistakes. Critics of our national legislature often try to paint it as aloof from the cares of Americans, a distant and unapproachable institution. In fact, the opposite is true: Congress is highly responsive to pressure. Sometimes that pressure comes from all directions, as people in every walk of life weigh in on a matter they care about deeply; sometimes it comes from a single source that no one else much notices.

In many cases, this process has produced laws and innovations of which we can rightly be proud. But sometimes it results in Congress approving legislation that doesn't pass the test of time. Our founders made Congress a deliberative body in which legislation can take months and even years to pass in large part because they were aware of this and wanted to make it difficult for Congress to head off in a misguided direction. Even so, it happens.

In fact, it's not hard to come up with a long list of congressional actions—or cases of inaction—that with hindsight look quite unfortunate. Take this country's history of mistreating Native Americans through policies that were set by Congress. High protective tariffs in the 1930s, passed by Congress to protect various U.S. industries, deepened and lengthened the Great Depression. Prohibition passed in 1919, only to be repealed a decade and a half—and many violent episodes—later. Our failure after World War I to ratify the treaty setting up the League of Nations stemmed from Congress's decision not to engage the world through an international organization, a judgment that in retrospect may have helped usher in World War II. In the past ten years, Congress has frequently sidestepped difficult issues, doing little about the large number of Americans without health insurance, the long-term threats to the solvency of Social Security, and our dependence on foreign energy sources.

There are plenty of reasons Congress gets things wrong. Sometimes its workload is so heavy that issues don't get the thorough consideration they need. Sometimes the questions it takes up are so complex, and the competing interests are so diverse, that honest attempts at legislating a solution will fail. Sometimes there are political calculations or trade-offs that produce less-than-perfect results. And sometimes Congress is simply trying to develop policies that it thinks reflect the interests and desires of specific groups of people, yet do not serve the interests of all the people. It is a reminder that Congress—for whatever reason—makes mistakes, even with procedures and motivations that in other circumstances can produce solid results.

One of the most enduring features of the legislative process is that issues are revisited again and again. Even when Congress acts in the right way—such as passing Title IX to ensure that women are treated fairly in college programs and athletics—it still needs to go back later to make sure everything is working properly. Hence the appropriate review recently of whether Title IX has had any unintended consequences on men's athletics, exploring whether any adjustments or refinements might be needed. The same is true when Congress makes a mistake and gets something wrong. It needs to go back to the issue again and again, reassessing the options, trying to develop a sounder policy. All of this reinforces the point that the work of Congress is never settled once and for all but is always being revisited and refined.

Members of Congress Who Had an Impact

A few years back, *Roll Call,* which is a bit like the hometown newspaper for Capitol Hill, published a list of the ten most important members of Congress in the twentieth century. It included some familiar names—Lyndon Johnson, Hubert Humphrey, Robert Taft—and some names that people with a knowledge of American history would recognize, such as Joseph Cannon, the iron-fisted

House Speaker in the early years of the twentieth century, and Robert La Follette, the founder of the Progressive movement. As I read the article, though, I couldn't help but ponder how difficult creating the list must have been.

It's not fashionable these days to think of members of Congress as being influential. Sure, they might do something important for your community or have some authority within their committees on Capitol Hill. But many people would argue that, other than funding that handy new highway bypass or post office, the work of specific legislators has limited impact on the lives of Americans.

With all due respect, I disagree. Choosing ten names for the *Roll Call* article must have been difficult because it takes almost no effort at all to come up with a long list of members of Congress who have profoundly reshaped the lives of Americans, even going back into earlier periods of our country's history:

• In the very first session of Congress, for example, Virginia representative James Madison largely drafted and steered to passage the Bill of Rights, the first ten amendments to the Constitution which were ratified by the states in 1791.

• When he was speaker of the House from 1823 to 1825, Henry Clay of Kentucky developed his "American System" of national improvements, including a network of highways and waterways that greatly facilitated the movement of goods from farms and factories.

• In 1843, Representative Francis Smith of Maine led the effort to provide funds to Samuel Morse to develop a telegraph between Washington, D.C., and Baltimore, laying the groundwork for today's telecommunications industry. It was in an office in the Capitol that Morse a year later tapped out his famous message: "What hath God wrought!"

• During the mid-1800s, Congress was active in the expansion of the American territory. In 1859, Senator William Gwin of California first proposed to Russia the sale of Alaska to the United States.

• The nation's land-grant college and university system was created in 1862 through the work of Senator Justin Smith Morrill from Vermont, opening up higher education to the working class. That was 140 years ago, and yet there are hundreds of thousands of young people today who, were it not for Morrill's efforts, would have a much harder time getting a college degree.

• In one of the earliest efforts to protect America's stunning natural resources, Senator Samuel Clarke Pomeroy of Kansas led the effort in Congress in 1872 to set aside 2 million acres at Yellowstone as a public park for the benefit of the people.

• There isn't an American consumer who doesn't owe a debt to Senator John Sherman of Ohio, whose 1890 Sherman Antitrust Act opened up competition by eliminating business conspiracies that seek to monopolize the marketplace.

• Outraged by the looting of Indian cliff dwellings in the Southwest, Representative John Lacey of Iowa developed the 1906 Antiquities Act to protect battlefields, forts, canyons, and birthplaces of famous Americans as national monuments.

• In 1916, Representative Edward Keating of Colorado and Senator Robert L. Owen of Oklahoma were appalled by the widespread use of young children to work in manufacturing and industrial plants. Their Keating-Owen Act was the first federal effort to end child labor.

Other notable legislators since then include the following:

• Representative John Jacob Rogers of Massachusetts, whose efforts in 1924 led to the creation of the U.S. Foreign Service, giving the United States a well-trained network of diplomats all over the world;

• Representative Sam Rayburn of Texas and Senator George Norris of Nebraska, who brought about passage of the 1936 Rural Electrification Act, transforming the lives of millions of Americans;

• Representative Mary Norton from New Jersey, whose work as chair of the House Committee on Labor helped bring about passage of the 1938 Fair Labor Standards Act, setting the first national minimum wage;

• Senators Lister Hill from Alabama and Harold Burton of Ohio, whose 1946 act led to widespread construction of hospitals, particularly in rural areas, after World War II;

• Representatives Hale Boggs of Louisiana and George Fallon of Maryland, who shaped the 1956 Federal Interstate Highway Act, which has had an enormous impact on almost every facet of American life;

• Senators Hubert Humphrey of Minnesota and Everett Dirksen of Illinois, who were the pivotal sponsors of the 1964 Civil Rights Act, the landmark legislation that opened the door to racial equality in the United States;

• Representative Edith Green of Oregon, often called the "mother of higher education," whose Higher Education Act of 1965 created the federal student aid program, which has helped millions of undergraduates over the years.

The list could go on. But here's what makes selecting notable members of Congress even trickier. Working on specific pieces of legislation that change the country is important, but so is working to improve the institution of Congress itself. In the end, Congress is where the American people express themselves in all their diversity and come to some agreement on what to do about the problems of the day. If it doesn't work, then our republic doesn't work either. So to our brief survey I would add members of Congress who may not have a standout law bearing their name, but without whom we as a nation would be decidedly worse off:

• Richard Bolling, a brilliant Missourian who redesigned the federal budget process, making it far more thorough and accessible to the public, and whose knowledge of parliamentary procedure allowed him to push for congressional reforms over the years that made the institution itself far more responsive to the American people;

• Arthur Vandenberg, who exemplified bipartisanship by helping a president of the opposite party enact the Marshall Plan for European reconstruction;

- Carl Albert, a conciliator skilled at crafting compromises;
- Margaret Chase Smith, known for her courageous stand against the McCarthy hearings and their damaging impact on the institution of the Senate;
- Tip O'Neill, who defined the modern Speakership and knew how to make the system work;
- Mike Mansfield, Bill Gray, and Lindy Boggs—bridge builders who recognized the importance of developing consensus.

The American political system is built to move slowly so that Congress can guard against hasty action, take the time it needs to gain public acceptance for courageous legislation, and balance carefully the disparate forces in the country. Working within such a system is not easy. It takes enormous political skill to forge majorities, make the necessary trade-offs, assuage egos, and accommodate the different points of view. All of the legislators I've mentioned here—and many others like them—were able to manage that process. If Congress did not have people like them, the American political system would not work. I can't think of any greater measure of influence.

3

How Congress Works

WE HAVE ALL SEEN SURVEYS like those showing that 66 percent of Americans can name the hosts of various game shows but only 6 percent can name the Speaker of the House, and those finding that large numbers of high school seniors believe that big states have more U.S. senators than small states. Americans are busy people with many demands on their time, and it is not easy to put in a full day's work or finish hours of homework and then read an article about Congress or turn on C-SPAN to watch the House or Senate in session.

As a member of Congress I was never particularly disturbed by such survey results dealing with some of the basic facts about Congress. After all, more than one politician has been tripped up on the campaign trail by questions about some basic fact of everyday life, such as the price of a gallon of milk. What did bother me, though, was the extent to which people didn't understand or appreciate some of the basic concepts that underlie the workings of Congress. Even if you don't know the number of your state's senators or representatives, you should know something about what they do. Even if you don't know all the steps in the legislative process, you should understand something about the notions of developing consensus and reaching compromise in our system of government. If too many Americans get those sorts of concepts wrong, it *does* matter to the health of our system of representative democracy. This chapter will explore some of the basics about what a member of Congress does and how Congress really works—a view from the inside.

A Complex Institution

Seeing news clips of congressional bickering or stories about congressional gridlock, many Americans must wonder why anyone would want to work there. That puzzlement has been long-standing. "It's easy to see why a man goes to the poorhouse or the penitentiary," a nineteenth-century observer of Congress noted. "It's because he can't help it. But why he should voluntarily go live in Washington is beyond my comprehension."[1] Yet to those of us who have been privileged to serve in Congress, it is a fascinating and vital institution.

Since the very first Congress in 1789, some twelve thousand men and women have served in the House or Senate. Over the years, its members have ranged from framers of our Constitution and frontier explorers to astronauts and Internet entrepreneurs. From its ranks have come twenty-four of our forty-three presidents and twenty-eight Supreme Court justices. I was always struck by the varied backgrounds of my fellow members. It would not be unusual to sit in a committee meeting with congressional colleagues who were once physicians, corporate CEOs, university professors, welfare recipients, social workers, professional athletes, physicists, or decorated war heroes. Former members of Congress invariably say one of the things they miss most is the daily interaction with their colleagues.

Congress is in many ways like a small city. More than thirty thousand people work in Congress, including auditors, legislative attorneys, caseworkers, library researchers, and Capitol police. Its buildings on Capitol Hill are spread over a forty-block, 250–acre complex, and most are connected by a labyrinth of corridors and underground tunnels. The Capitol building alone covers four acres. Its spaces range from the dramatic vistas of the West Front, where presidential inaugurations are held every four years, to the hidden, nearly inaccessible Intelligence Committee rooms, secure from even the most sophisticated electronic eavesdropping equipment.

Over more than two centuries, Congress has debated the structure of the new government, protective tariffs, Manifest Destiny, slavery and states' rights, declarations of war, civil rights and voting rights, articles of impeachment, and globalization. The main work of Congress is passing the nation's laws. In each two-year session, some five thousand bills will be introduced on the House side. And a comparable number of bills—often counterparts to House bills—will be introduced in the Senate. By the end of the two years, some five hundred new laws will be enacted, many of which will have multiple provisions incorporating several ideas originally introduced as individual bills.

Congress has two hundred committees and subcommittees to consider and prepare legislation, and members vote several hundred times each year on everything from routine procedural matters to resolutions of war or bills costing hundreds of billions of dollars. The variety of topics that come before Congress today is staggering, and moving bills requires a thorough understanding of a complicated legislative process with its own terminology—"mark-ups," "holds," "amendment trees," "filibusters," "cloture," "germaneness," "soft-earmarks," "suspension," "reconciliation," "PAYGO sequestration." When I entered the House, I was told in no uncertain terms to be quiet for my first few years until I understood Congress's rules and customs. Today's members become very active sooner, but there is still a fairly steep learning curve.

An Evolving Institution

Not fully appreciated is the extent to which Congress is an ever-changing, evolving institution. True, the core aspects of being a member of Congress have remained much the same since its first session more than two hundred years ago. If representatives or senators from an early Congress could be here today, they would still understand and appreciate the basics of congressional policy-making: the introduction of bills, the floor debate, the amending process, the House-Senate compromise, the possible presidential veto. They would understand the system's checks and balances and the important role Congress plays as the nation's premier forum for addressing the economic, social, and political issues of the day.

Yet many aspects of Congress have changed over the years, especially in the last several decades. During my years in the House I witnessed several major changes:

• *An expanded workload:* The workload of Congress has increased significantly over the years. Since I went to the House in 1965, the number of constituents that each House member represents has jumped by 40 percent, to an average of 650,000. The number of days in session, the number of recorded votes, the communications with lobbyists and constituents—all have increased sharply. Congress now receives 50 million e-mail messages and 200 million pieces of mail annually, compared with 10 million letters a year in the 1960s. The fax machines never stop running, and the phones never stop ringing. In my early years in Congress, I had one person handle all the correspondence; now most offices have five or six. And today Congress tackles a host of issues that didn't even exist in the 1960s—direct satellite broadcasting, ozone depletion, HMOs, cloning, AIDS research, computer privacy.

• *Budget process reform:* One of Congress's most important powers is its ability to set the spending and taxing policies of the nation. It seems hard to imagine now, but before 1970 Congress usually passed tax and spending measures without worrying much about their overall impact on the government's bottom line. The executive branch kept an accounting of whether the government ran a surplus or fell into a deficit at the end of each fiscal year. That changed in the 1970s, when Congress approved a series of budget-process reforms. Since then, lawmakers have made their decisions about spending in a much more coordinated and coherent way, with a close eye on how their decisions will affect, and be affected by, the economy.

• *A more complicated legislative process:* The movement of legislation through the congressional maze has never been more complicated, largely because Congress has made some major changes to the way it does business. In some cases, members have devised methods to circumvent the regular order, so they can move some bills through with minimal examination by their colleagues—including huge omnibus bills packaging together thousands of provisions and presented for just an up or down vote. In other cases, they have added procedural layers through their budget-process reforms, generating more points of order and additional motions and amendments. Filibusters, both formal and informal, have increased greatly in recent decades, which means the Senate now basically requires sixty votes to get anything done rather than a simple majority of 51. And the use of ad hoc committees to deal with special problems has greatly expanded, with the effect of further fragmenting responsibility for legislative issues.

• *Ethics reform:* Congress has tightened its ethics standards, an improvement that receives little public attention. When I came to the House, there were no financial disclosure requirements for members, no restrictions on accepting gifts or using campaign contributions for personal use, no written code of conduct, and no standing ethics committees to police the membership. All that has changed with a series of major reforms, primarily in the 1970s, which I was pleased to have played a role in helping to shape. Moreover, due to the well-trained eye of the media lens, members face more scrutiny than ever of their personal finances, campaign contributions, and office accounts. We have made important strides in reinforcing ethical behavior, though more certainly needs to be done.

• *Increased openness:* Congress has opened its proceedings in recent years, which is a bracing change. In 1965 no recorded votes were permitted on floor votes on amendments, so people had to be stationed in the House gallery to try to figure out how members were voting on controversial measures. That meant, for example, that we had to do a lot of thinking about how to get a recorded vote on the Vietnam War. At the time, the only way to oppose the war was to vote against the entire defense bill, which made it difficult for me because, although I had doubts about the war, I supported defense. It took a long time, but we finally passed procedural reforms that required roll-call votes on amendments. Today, House and Senate floor action is televised gavel to gavel, and votes are computerized so they are quickly and broadly accessible on the Internet. Some of Congress's key decisions are still being made behind closed doors, but almost all committee proceedings are open, and many are carried live on cable television or the Internet.

• *The decline in civility:* One of the more disturbing changes I've witnessed since 1965 has been the decline in civility among members. Certainly the history of Congress has been marked by rough periods, but too often in recent years politics has meant bitter partisan exchanges and mean personal attacks. We have sometimes seen more emphasis on questioning motives than on debating the pros and cons of the issue itself. One member coming off the House floor summed it up simply: "Man, it's rough out there." Spirited debate is appropriate, even healthy, and Congress remains a safe forum in which the conflicts within our society can be aired. But antagonism, incivility, and the tendency to demonize opponents all make it very difficult for members to come together to pass legislation for the good of the country.

• *A more representative Congress:* Congress reflects our country's diversity better today than in past decades, with far more blacks, women, Hispanics, and Asian Americans among its members, particularly in the House. Although further progress is needed, Congress is still one of the most representative institutions in the country. This change has directly affected congressional policymaking. In recent years, for example, there have been more than seventy women in Congress, compared with thirteen when I entered the House, and they have pushed to the forefront issues like gender discrimination, sexual harassment, breast cancer research, and family leave. Few politicians today would give a speech without saying something about the family, a major policy theme that only developed after women came into Congress. Almost certainly their numbers will continue to grow.

• *Electronic access:* During my early years in Congress, congressional offices used telephones, typewriters with carbon paper, and thermal faxes, which would transmit somewhat legible documents at a rate of three or four minutes per page (when they worked). Today's Congress takes advantage of the latest advances of the information age, and a new form of "electronic democracy" seems to be emerging. Individual members use websites, e-mail, satellite hookups, video conferencing, and chat rooms to communicate with constituents about what's going on in Congress. Some have set up live, interactive "virtual town meetings" via the Internet. On the various congressional websites, people can take a virtual tour of Congress, learn about the legislative process, obtain House and Senate documents, track the status of every bill moving through Congress, see live webcasts of hearings, and download hundreds of research reports on the major issues before Congress.

Over the next decades Congress will continue to change in ways we cannot predict or even imagine today. But it will still remain the protector of our freedom and the premier forum for addressing the key issues of the day.

The Many Roles of a Member of Congress

Ask most people what their member of Congress does on a typical day at work, and they're likely to say that he or she gives speeches, votes on issues, and sometimes shows up on TV or in the newspapers. Members do these things, to be sure, but that's just a fraction of what the job involves.

If someone were putting together a "Help Wanted" ad for the job of congressman, most members of Congress would say it would read something like this: "Wanted: Person with wide-ranging knowledge of scores of complex public policy issues. Must be willing to work long hours in Washington, then fly home to attend an unending string of community events. Applicant should expect that work and travel demands will strain family life, and that every facet of public and private life will be subject to intense scrutiny and criticism."

Being in Congress is hardly a lousy job. To the contrary, I found my work deeply fulfilling. But there were certainly times when I was frustrated by how little my constituents understood what I did and what the institution was all about. For all the media coverage of Congress, what members do on a daily basis still remains somewhat of a mystery to most people, even though several of those roles might be of particular benefit to them. Article 1 of the Constitution sets forth the powers of Congress and the qualifications necessary for election, but it contains no discussion of specific duties for the individual member. So in a sense members shape their own priorities. Yet they typically perform at least a dozen major roles:

• *National legislator:* Members spend a considerable amount of time on legislative duties, working to pass the laws of the nation and to determine federal spending levels for thousands of programs. During my years in Congress, the range of federal programs grew considerably, and a member's legislative responsibilities grew more complex and time-consuming. Our five hundred votes per year would cover a mind-boggling array of issues, from stem-cell research to education funding to human cloning to global warming. In the *Federalist,* James Madison wrote that a member of Congress needed to understand just three issues: commerce, taxation, and the militia. To a legislator today, that observation is a bit quaint, to say the least.

• *Local representative:* Each member represents his or her constituents in Congress. That means monitoring and seeking their opinions, recognizing their priorities, interests, and economic needs, and then trying to make sure that legislation passed by Congress reflects those perspectives. The founders were very clear that they wanted input from all regions of the country as Congress considered legislation.

• *Constituent advocate:* A member of Congress must be an advocate and ombudsman for individuals, groups, industries, and communities back home. This means everything from helping a senior who is having problems getting a Social Security check to helping a community obtain federal funding for a major new road. Because it's often difficult to figure out which local, state, or federal agency can help with a particular problem, people often start by asking their congressman. And as the federal government has expanded over the years, serving constituents and communities has become more far-reaching and time-consuming. In fact, members of Congress will sometimes complain that constituent service is crowding out the time they need to study legislation on which they must vote.

• *Committee member:* Committee work is one of the key duties in Washington. Each House member typically serves on two committees and each senator four, as well as several subcommittees. The point that Woodrow Wilson made many years ago—"Congress in session is Congress on public exhibition, whilst Congress in its committee-rooms is Congress at work"—is still largely true.[2] Although members must be generalists to be able to vote on the broad range of issues before Congress, they also tend to specialize in the areas handled by their committees, and develop considerable expertise in these areas.

• *Investigator:* Congress is charged with overseeing the operation of the federal government and in particular with ensuring that the president and the federal departments and agencies are carrying out efficiently and effectively the policies Congress has approved. This can mean everything from discovering that the Pentagon is spending six hundred dollars for a toilet seat to making sure U.S. intelligence operations are getting the right information to the right people at the right time. This work tends to be time-consuming and tedious, and pays few political dividends to individual members, but regular oversight of the implementation of laws stands at the very core of good government.

• *Educator:* Being in Congress also means being an educator, translating the work of Congress to constituents in an accessible, understandable way—sometimes through the media, most often directly. To be effective in this role, a member of Congress needs to establish a rapport with all types of people, from factory workers to white-collar professionals, from senior citizens to young students. I don't know of another job that puts you in closer touch with people—all kinds of people—than the job of a member of Congress.

• *Student:* At the same time, a member of Congress must also be a student of the views of his or her constituents. I quickly learned that no matter what the subject, there was always a constituent who knew more about it than I did.

• *Local dignitary:* A member of Congress must perform the ceremonial function of dignitary at home, serving as the "ambassador" from the nation's capital. The invitations never stop arriving, and literally 365 days a year could be filled attending community events back home. I often joked with constituents that I had been in more parades (thirty or more for thirty-four years) than any living American. If a member does not keep up a high profile at home, local wags say that he's come down with "Potomac fever" and forgotten the folks who elected him.

• *Fund-raiser:* As the cost of running for reelection has risen sharply—in my own case, it went from $30,000 in my first race to $1 million in my last—members have had to spend more and more time raising funds for their campaigns. To put this in perspective, running a $1 million campaign means that over the two years in a House term, you have to raise $10,000 from contributors every week.

• *Staff manager:* House members manage an average of seventeen personal staffers, while senators have forty. These aides work on Capitol Hill primarily on legislative matters, and in district or state offices mostly on casework and local projects. In addition, many members supervise committee staff, and those running for reelection also have separate campaign staffs. At one point, I had more than eighty staff people working for me.

• *Party leader:* Members are active in their party's caucus in Congress, attending meetings, helping to formulate a common position on pending issues, and working on strategies for the passage of particularly important legislative priorities. At home, members are involved in supporting local party tickets, broadening the party's base of support, and motivating voters.

• *Consensus builder:* The most effective members of Congress are skilled at bringing people together and finding mutually agreeable solutions to the various challenges facing our nation. It is extremely difficult in our diverse nation to forge consensus on complicated and controversial issues, and the tough work of hammering out compromise is almost impossible to accomplish in front of the TV lights. Those who are good at it often don't get public credit, since it's a job that is best done behind the scenes, in personal meetings with other members and their staff. Yet it is essential to the proper functioning of our system of government.

The demands on a member of Congress can be many and the personal moments few. But through these various roles, members receive an enormous amount of satisfaction in the part they have played in making the lives of people better and the country stronger.

Representing Constituents

Despite the complexity of Congress and its members' many roles, at its most basic the core responsibilities of members of Congress are two: passing and overseeing legislation, and representing their constituents. The framers of the Constitution viewed Congress as the country's policymaking engine and gave it broad legislative powers. Yet Congress is not only a legislative institution but also a representative one. Members are asked not just to pass laws but also to represent in Washington the interests of the districts and states they serve.

Thus one of the most perennially distressing poll results is the view that members don't care what ordinary citizens think. Polls consistently show that more than three-fifths of the public do not expect public officials to be responsive to their thoughts. In a 1996 survey, almost *half* of the respondents said they thought members of Congress would pay very little or no attention if they contacted them.

When I hear this, I often think of a conversation I had with Wilbur Mills, an enormously powerful legislator from Arkansas who had long chaired the House Ways and Means Committee. One evening we walked out of the Capitol together after a vote. His picture was on the cover of *TIME*, and he was known all over the country for his power over the tax code and his role in setting up Medicare. Powerful people sought his advice and clamored to speak with him even for a few seconds. I asked him where he was going and he said, "I'm going back to Arkansas. I'm holding a public meeting." He mentioned some small Arkansas town and said, "There'll be about fifteen or twenty people there." As we parted he said, "Lee, don't ever forget your constituents. Nothing, nothing comes before them." I never forgot it.

Having served with thousands of members over the years, my clear sense is that this attitude is the norm, not the exception. Members and their staffs put enormous effort into staying in touch with constituents back home, and they are probably more attuned to what their constituents think than at any time in the past. Most of them know their home turf very well. They know who its employers are, where its plants are located, and where people go for coffee in the morning; and they take frequent trips home to spend time in those places. A good friend of mine liked simply to head for the local shopping mall, where he would set up a table and listen to any comments people might have. Another made a habit of setting up a mobile office in the parking lot outside his state university's football stadium on game weekends. Members hold numerous public meetings, poll their districts regularly, and answer scores of letters and e-mail messages daily. They're on the telephone every day just to check up with constituents, and the door is always open to visitors from back home. Aware that the next election is never far off, members want to avoid being accused of "losing touch."

Besides, the vast majority of members are "of the community." Their roots—and often a large number of family members and close friends—are there, and they still maintain a residence in their home state. They know the area intimately because it is where they are from, and they have no desire to make decisions that will harm "their people" back home.

So why this impression that elected officials aren't representing the voices of common folk? Part of it, I suspect, is the general mistrust of politicians that marks this era in our history. Part of it, too, is that as districts grow larger and more diverse and as the issues besetting our country become more complex, it becomes harder for a member of Congress to know with assurance what constituents think about any single issue. But the biggest problem is that there is often little agreement among constituents on a given question. People often think that most of their fellow citizens agree with them about what is right and necessary, and they see no good reason why Congress shouldn't enact their point of view. Yet the fact is, it is very difficult to get agreement among a broad cross-section of Americans on any current major political issue.

Surveys over the years have shown that Americans don't even agree on what are the most important issues facing the country, let alone the best way to solve them. True, Congress was able to act forcefully in the 1960s to pass major civil rights legislation and more recently to respond to the September 11 attack, a reflection of the broad consensus that existed in the country. But in most years, when people are asked to identify the country's most important problem, they're all over the map. In a 1998 survey, for example, most of the respondents thought there was substantial agreement among Americans on the most important problem facing the nation. Yet when asked to identify it, no more than 10 percent of the respondents agreed on any single item.[3]

My own sense is that, if anything, members may be too responsive to constituents, paying attention to every shift in local opinion and every blip in the polls and thinking more about what's popular with their constituents than about what's good for the country as a whole. Abraham Lincoln once said that the art of democratic government is to be out in front of your constituents, but not too far out in front. Members are sometimes too close to their constituents, particularly when they risk reflecting their constituents' views at the expense of their own considered judgment—for example, going along with the popular conviction that Social Security should never be tinkered with, even when reform is clearly needed to prevent the program's long-term insolvency.

This is not a popular view. As one irate constituent shouted to his representative, "We didn't send you to Washington to make intelligent decisions. We sent you to represent us."[4]

But the founders didn't believe that Congress should simply mirror the will of the people. They believed it ought to "refine and enlarge the public view." They thought that members should favor the *national* interest in their deliberations. Yet it is not clear it has worked that way, as most members lean toward a local orientation, emphasizing their representative function. That's why people like their own representatives and senators, with well over 90 percent of those running again getting reelected. But it is also why national legislation aimed at the common good can get derailed for parochial interests, and why public opinion of Congress as an institution is fairly low. This basic tension between the representative and legislative functions of members has been going on for more than two hundred years, and it still remains today.

How a Bill Really Becomes Law

When I visit with students in American government classes, I always make a point of flipping through their textbooks to see the diagram illustrating "How a Bill Becomes a Law" in Washington. The diagram explains that a piece of legislation, once introduced, moves through subcommittee and committee, then to the House and Senate floors, then to a House-Senate conference, and finally to the president for his signature or veto.

Such diagrams can at times be helpful. But my basic reaction is: "How boring! How sterile!" The diagram can't possibly convey the challenges, the hard work, the obstacles to be overcome, the defeats suffered, the victories achieved, and the sheer excitement that attend the legislative process. It gives a woefully incomplete picture of how complicated and untidy that process can be, and barely hints at the difficulties facing any member of Congress who wants to shepherd an idea into law.

You don't just have an idea, draft it in bill form, and drop it in the House hopper or file it at the Senate desk. Developing the idea is very much a political process—listening to the needs and desires of people and then trying to translate that into a specific legislative proposal. Even the earliest stages of drafting a bill involve much maneuvering. The member needs to consult with colleagues, experts, and interest groups to refine and sharpen the idea; gauge the political impact and viability of the proposal (especially with constituents); determine how to formulate the idea so it appeals to a majority of colleagues; study how it differs from and improves upon related proposals introduced in the past; decide how broadly or narrowly to draft it (to avoid it being referred to too many committees); and decide how to draft it so it gets sent to a sympathetic rather than an unsympathetic committee. The Civil Rights Act of 1964, for example, succeeded because it was carefully drafted to avoid the Senate Judiciary Committee, where it would most likely have died; instead, its wording triggered a referral to the more agreeable Commerce Committee. To do this it avoided Fourteenth Amendment equal-protection arguments and instead relied on the federal government's power to regulate interstate commerce and in particular to prohibit discrimination in public accommodations—like motel and restaurant chains—that participated in interstate commerce.

Next, members don't simply introduce a good idea and then watch it move nicely through the legislative process. They need to rally support for the bill. The most time-consuming aspect of moving legislation is conversation: the scores—even hundreds—of one-on-one talks that an astute member will hold with colleagues to make the case for a particular bill, to learn what arguments opponents will use to try to block it, and to get a sense of what adjustments might be needed to move it along.

There was a time when it didn't take a hundred conversations to advance a proposal. If you could sell your idea to the leadership and one or two key committee chairmen, their clout would carry a bill well down the road to passage. Nowadays, though, more people on Capitol Hill have legislative power, including subcommittee chairmen, party leaders, leadership-appointed task forces, and individual members, especially those who are skilled at attracting media attention. You also need to consult people outside Congress, including key special interest groups who have much to gain or lose depending on the precise language of a bill and who have influence with members and extensive grassroots lobbying networks. Moving legislation today requires both an "inside" and an "outside" strategy—working to develop not only member interest but also public support. The media can be a powerful friend or a powerful adversary when trying to move legislation along.

Moreover, rather than expecting collegial acceptance of the idea, a member must be prepared to debate every line of a bill with his or her colleagues—certainly a formidable process but one that usually improves the final product. You need to develop the most persuasive arguments for the bill, be able to anticipate and respond to objections, consider which arguments or nonlegislative considerations might appeal to different colleagues, and find ways to demonstrate how the bill will help local districts.

The soundings from this smorgasbord of conversations generally wind up creating a dilemma: If you alter the proposal to accommodate skeptics you might broaden its appeal, but if you compromise too much you alienate core supporters. Successful legislators constantly count votes to ensure they have enough support, and they must be strategically savvy enough to determine whether they can mollify the opposition or must simply push ahead and hope to defeat it. They need to check with the parliamentarian to make sure that technical glitches do not undermine the bill. And they must consult regularly with congressional leaders, at a minimum to keep them advised if not actively involved. In the end it is the leadership that has the authority to make the vital decisions on when—or even if—to schedule a bill for floor debate and a chance at a vote on final passage.

All this adds up to a process that is extremely dynamic, messy, and unpredictable. There are ways for astute or powerful members to get around nearly every stage in the traditional model of the legislative process, making those "How a Bill Becomes a Law" charts of little value in predicting the path of legislation.

If with conversation, persuasion, persistence, and luck, a House member clears the many hurdles and gets a bill passed by that chamber, the reward is to begin the difficult journey anew in the Senate, where the threat of a filibuster immensely complicates the legislative process. Unless sixty of one hundred senators vote to close off debate on a measure, it is effectively blocked; the Senate on many issues no longer operates by simple majority rule.

The fate of a legislative proposal is also influenced by the preferences of the president and the executive branch bureaucracy. A member of Congress trying to advance a bill must take constant readings from the White House to learn if the president will veto it or sign it in its current form.

Guiding a bill from proposal to law requires energy, persistence, and competence. The legislative process is far from mechanical or automatic. Instead, it is dynamic, fluid, and unpredictable, with the outcome very much affected by the players—their goals, skills, ingenuity, and temperament. A skillful legislator must understand not only the basic mechanics of the process but also the personalities, the politics, and the strategies in order to succeed.

The workings of Washington sometimes appear to be a tangled and contentious maze, but there is a basic framework in which the action takes place. Granted, it is not as tidy as the textbook diagrams suggest; the legislative process is increasingly complex and dynamic and thoroughly political from beginning to end. But the structures through which a bill must pass have been set up to enhance the representative functions of Congress, with legislative efficiency taking a back seat. It is a process that goes to extraordinary lengths to take into account the need to hear from all points of view and to build consensus. Rarely is that quick or neat work, but it is the fundamental stuff of democracy, and it has served our country well.

Why We Need More Politicians

What this country really needs is more politicians! That was one thing I used to say to groups that was sure to get a reaction. When the snickers died down, I would explain that I was actually quite serious, that we do need more people who know how to practice the art of politics.

This is not a skill that has come in for much praise in recent years, but that's because we're confused about what it entails. When the federal government almost shut down a few years back, that was considered "politics." When Washington grew obsessed with the impeachment of President Clinton and the rest of the people's business took a back seat, that was "politics." Showing skill as "a politician" has come to mean demonstrating the ability to raise campaign funds, or to engage in the tit-for-tat exchange of negative advertising, or to jockey for public support based on polls and focus groups, or to skewer an opponent with a one-liner during a televised debate.

So we've come to view the word "politician" with considerable disdain. Yet none of this defines a good politician. Good politicians are vital to the functioning of our democracy, and we desperately need more of them. Let me give you an example of what I mean.

Suppose you're in Congress, and you decide to start focusing on our country's drug problem. Let's say, as well, that you firmly believe the answer lies in using federal funds to back more treatment programs for addicts. But then an interesting thing happens. As you talk to your colleagues, you discover that they're all over the map on the issue: Some support hard jail time for users; some want to beef up antidrug education efforts; some want to help law officers or to strengthen border patrols; others want funding for medical research into the causes of addiction; and still others want to focus on eradicating crops in Asia and South America. Gradually, it begins to dawn on you that to make progress on the issue, you're going to have to find a way to give others some of what they want as well. It's at this moment, as you set about crafting a bill that can take all these voices into account, that you'll begin to discover why true politics is considered an art.

There are plenty of people who would look at the process of reconciling these competing points of view as messy and unseemly. "Stick to your guns!" they would urge. "Anything less is a sell-out." But controversy and conflict in a large nation are unavoidable. To avoid ripping apart at the seams, our country needs people who know how to accommodate different points of view and work for common solutions. That is what good politicians do: They make democratic government possible in a nation alive with competing factions. Simply put, they make the country work.

Hardly anyone appreciates this. As we scrutinize members of Congress, we all but ignore their political skills. In the many years I represented southern Indiana in Congress, I participated in thousands of public forums, newspaper and television interviews, and radio call-in shows. But I can count on one hand the number of times I was asked questions that dealt with my political skills. People knew where I stood on expanding trade and helping seniors; they even knew I shared the Hoosier passion for basketball. But for the most part, they never asked me how good I would be at turning their concerns or mine into law or at advancing local and state interests among my 534 colleagues in Congress. For some reason most people and journalists seem to take basic political competence for granted.

They shouldn't. As hard as it is to get to Congress, doing a good job once you're there is even harder. The key is respecting the system and figuring out how to make it work. Frequently you will find people in Congress with high ideals, good ideas, and considerable energy, who nonetheless lose because they never figured out how to work the system to get things done. It takes being a good politician, in the best sense of the word: that in the face of the diverse beliefs and opinions represented in Washington, you can work with your colleagues to build support for an idea and move it forward.

So what should we be looking for in a politician, someone who is able to practice the art of politics in Congress?

First, they should know how to consult, particularly with their fellow members—talking to them, listening to them, making sure they feel they are in the loop. You build support for ideas one-on-one with colleagues and key individuals. They all have their own ideas and their own valid concerns; they expect to be able to share them, not simply to be lectured to. Lyndon Johnson had his own way of putting this, with the sign he had in his Senate office: "You ain't learning nothing when you're talking." Good politicians need to be able to hear from all sides, and they soon realize that you can never consult sufficiently.

Second, they should be able to calm rather than inflame the discussion of controversial issues. In public meetings in Indiana and in discussions in Congress, I often encountered people who were angry or felt passionately about a particular issue and might end up shedding more heat than light on an issue. I didn't always agree with my colleagues, but I tried to make sure the disagreements were honestly stated, orderly, and civil. I remember Carl Albert telling us to always respect our colleagues and never forget that each of them serves in this House because they were elected to do so by the American people.

Third, they should know how to persuade. It takes an enormous amount of work to build a majority's support for an idea. I once set out to push a modest piece of legislation having to do with reviewing the operations of Congress. It wasn't especially complicated, but by the time I was done trying to line up support, I'd been in touch with more than a hundred individuals from both parties.

Fourth, they should be willing to share the credit. I remember former Speaker Tip O'Neill putting his arm around me as we walked down the hall and giving me some advice. He called me Neal for my first decade in Congress because I reminded him of a Boston baseball player by the name of Neal Hamilton. "Neal," he said, "you can accomplish anything in this town if you're willing to let someone else take the credit."

Finally, they should know how to compromise. The public and the press try to lock members of Congress into more and more specific positions on the issues, well in advance of a vote. But good politicians search for the common ground among diverse views and know how to make adjustments to their proposals without betraying their core beliefs. One of the most misunderstood concepts in our system of government is the notion of compromise and reaching consensus, with polls showing most Americans think compromise just means selling out on your principles.

But compromise is essential to producing law in our system of representative democracy. Disagreements over views deeply held are unavoidable in a nation as large and diverse as the United States, and people will inevitably differ over means and ends. Good politicians are able to find the points of agreement that will allow a consensus to emerge, looking for solutions that allow both sides to claim, if not victory, at least some gains. It might be altering some key words, phasing in a change, inserting a new provision, requiring a study, splitting differences in funding, delaying or postponing implementation of a section. There is almost always a way to solve problems without confrontation, and part of the skill of a member of Congress is finding ways to resolve differences. Skillful legislators seek accommodations among rival interests, because they know that it's necessary to make the country work. Other issues will surely come along, and good politicians recognize that creating permanent enemies will make it difficult, if not impossible, to enlist their help in the future.

Of all the skills demanded of an effective member of Congress, developing consensus—bringing people together, accommodating different points of view, and finding acceptable solutions to our nation's problems—is perhaps the most important of all. It is why we need more politicians these days, not fewer.

Power in Congress

Central to being an effective member and moving legislation through Congress is understanding who has the real power in the institution. Sometimes it takes time to master an institutional nuance about power; sometimes you get the point rather quickly.

I remember getting a vivid introduction to how power works on Capitol Hill as a freshman member of Congress. Following the lead of the president, a small group of us introduced a measure to extend the term of House members from two years to four. Given its support in the White House, we thought we had a chance for success, so we were optimistic when we approached the chairman of the House Judiciary Committee, an awesome and fearsome New Yorker named Emanuel Celler. I was designated the spokesman for the group. How, I wanted to know, did Mr. Celler stand on the bill?

"I don't stand on it," he responded. "I'm sitting on it. It rests four-square under my fanny and will never see the light of day." He was right. It didn't. And we learned that day something about congressional power—that some individuals have enormous power within the institution either to move legislation forward or to kill it.

Whenever national attention focuses on Congress, it's crucial to remember that power is not equally shared within its walls. To understand why some proposals make it and some don't, you also have to understand who has the real power in Congress.

This is not quite as easy as it might seem. One of the most noteworthy features of congressional power is that it regularly shifts over time. In the nineteenth century, the Speaker of the House had enormous power over the membership, as you can gather from the nicknames of Speakers like "Czar" or "Boss." In the early twentieth century, a revolt by rank-and-file members shifted power to the committee chairmen, and in turn more power was given to individual members by the post-Watergate reforms of 1974. In the 1980s and 1990s, there was a sense that the decentralization of power had gone too far, and over the past decade the Speaker and his leadership team have once again become more powerful.

The truth is, though, that power in Congress shifts not only from one era to the next but also from one election to the next, as party strength and committee alignments change, and even from one issue to the next. One proposal might move through Congress because it's the priority of a powerful committee chair or is strongly supported by the administration. Another might move because its champion has a high media profile and the ability to command national support, even though he or she does not serve on the relevant committee. Yet another might pass because a determined voting bloc within Congress insists on its inclusion in exchange for their votes on the overall bill.

What makes Congress different from most institutions is that no one is in charge of the entire body. There is no CEO or person whose desk has a plaque reading, "The Buck Stops Here." There are easily identifiable leadership positions, of course, where the organizational charts tell you that power should reside. Yet despite their stature, their visibility in the media, and their ability to organize the chamber and schedule floor business, congressional leaders don't actually have much power to force members to act in a certain way. This is because Congress is highly decentralized, few members consider themselves followers, and the leaders do not have many formal powers to call upon. When he was Senate Majority Leader, Bob Dole would often say that a "p" was missing from his title—that he should have been called the Majority Pleader instead. When he was House Speaker, Carl Albert used to say, "I have no power but the power to persuade."

A basic truth in mathematics is that the whole is equal to the sum of the parts. Yet that has never applied to Congress. Members of Congress are a talented group overall, yet the institution itself doesn't seem to measure up to the sum of their individual talents. I'm not quite sure why that is, but part of the explanation might lie in the manner in which Congress is organized and power distributed.

The power of individual members comes from multiple sources. In the first instance, it derives from the fact of their election, which bestows a certain power both inside and outside the institution.

Obviously, it helps to hold a committee chairmanship or serve on particular committees, such as the "money" committees that in recent decades have become dominant on Capitol Hill—the Appropriations Committees, the House and Senate Budget Committees, and the Senate Finance and House Ways and Means Committees. But beyond that, particular members may be powerful because they are persuasive debaters or securely in command of the facts they need to convince others. They may be well liked or highly respected for their judgment or expertise. They may be media-savvy or close to the president or adept fund-raisers who can help out other members in their campaigns for reelection. In more recent days, the ability to raise campaign money has become the path to leadership and power in Congress. Power also rests in the hands of those who have effective political skills—the ability to listen, build coalitions, accommodate different points of view, and make compromises. And sometimes power grows out of members' experiences outside Congress—as Senator John McCain's years as a POW have given him enormous standing on defense issues—or because they speak for a major special interest group—as Claude Pepper once did for seniors.

Whatever its source, power is what moves ideas and legislative proposals along in Congress, and it is also what can slow them down. The key sources of power for every bill are different, as the mix of players involved constantly shifts, depending on the issue under consideration and the stage of the legislative process reached. All of this makes the legislative process very fluid, very dynamic, and endlessly fascinating.

The House and the Senate

People are surprised to hear that I authored one of the biggest, most comprehensive tax cut bills considered by Congress in the 1980s. Well, maybe not in the way you might expect.

Actually what happened was that I introduced a very minor bill, HR 5829, to provide some tax relief to the church I attended in

Washington, so they wouldn't have to pay high import duties on a new set of bells they had just imported from Europe. Under the division of responsibilities between the House and the Senate as laid out in the Constitution, only the House has the power to originate tax legislation. Since the Senate wanted very much to draft a major tax cut bill, particularly during the 1980 campaign year, they took my bill once it passed the House, basically deleted everything after the bill number, and in its place put their extensive tax cut language as an "amendment." So it was my modest HR 5829 which became the major vehicle in the Congress that year for debating tax cuts. My office obviously received more than a few puzzled calls about this. But the point is that the standard textbook lists of differences in roles and responsibilities between the House and Senate have become increasingly blurred in recent years.

Of all the changes in Congress since it was established more than two hundred years ago, the framers would probably be most surprised by how much the Senate has changed. The framers had divided up various powers and responsibilities between the House and the Senate, with the House, for example, originating revenue bills and the Senate approving treaties and presidential nominations. But they also viewed the two bodies as having two distinct roles in the basic legislative process: The House, whose members were elected every two years, was to be the closely connected to the needs, desires, and wishes of the American people and was to be the voice of popular opinion. The Senate, on the other hand, with its membership appointed by the states and with its six-year terms for senators, was to be the much more detached body that would take the legislation passed by the House reflecting popular passions and consider it in a more deliberative way.

The framers were very clear on the distinctive nature of the Senate. As George Washington explained, just as we pour coffee into a saucer to try to cool it down, "we pour legislation into the senatorial saucer to cool it."[5] Over the years, various changes to the Senate have eroded this key role, including ratification of the Seventeenth Amendment in 1913 providing that senators too would be elected by the people, thus making them much more responsive to popular opinion. It is still probably true, however, that House members tend to view themselves more as local officials—working on local projects, staying in close contact with county officials and mayors, emphasizing direct personal contact with the voters through scores of local town meetings—while senators tend to view themselves more as national figures. And House members are still generally more responsive to the latest blip in public opinion, while the Senate remains the more deliberative body.

Other differences between the two bodies range from the larger percentage of votes needed in the Senate to cut off debate and move a bill forward, to the tendency of senators to be generalists covering a broad range of legislative interests while House members tend to develop considerable expertise in the more focused areas covered by their committees. One of the more important differences relates to size. Because the House has many more members, House rules are stricter and give the majority party far greater power to move legislation. Floor consideration of legislation is generally highly structured in the House. The majority controls the procedures, and he who controls the procedure controls the results. If the majority party can hold its members together, the minority in the House is basically out of the game. On the other hand, individual senators—of both parties—have extensive powers in the legislative process, being able to debate any measure at length and to offer any amendments—even unrelated amendments—to whatever bill is under consideration. In general, House rules favor the majority—so the will of the people prevails without being blocked by the minority—while Senate rules give advantages to the minority so they can stop the majority from acting too quickly.

One constant is that each body continues to perceive the other as an obstacle to be overcome in the legislative process, with members often frustrated by the other chamber's procedures. Grumbling about the other body's handling of an important matter is commonplace. It's become almost a standing joke among members that it is the *other* body that is messing things up and is responsible for the ills of the legislative process. There is also a genuine competition between the two bodies—trying to be first to get the prominent witnesses, to move important legislation, to respond to national crises—which is by and large a healthy competition.

Most Americans take it for granted, but our truly bicameral system, with two chambers of equal power, sets Congress apart from almost any other parliament in the world today. The roles of the House and Senate may not be exactly the same as envisioned by the framers, but important differences remain, generally enhancing the overall workings of the Congress.

The Awesome Responsibility of Voting

As I was chatting with a constituent one day, he brought me up short with a simple question: "What's the toughest part of your job?" At the time, I'd represented southern Indiana in Congress for well over two decades, but I had to pause to sort through the possible answers. The long hours? The time spent away from home? The criticism? The heavy lobbying? Suddenly, it came to me that the answer had nothing to do with the frustrations of the job but with its essence: The toughest part of serving in Congress is voting on legislation.

Voting is an awesome responsibility, and it lies at the very heart of a member's duties. I remember my first vote as a new member in January 1965. It was to elect the Speaker of the House, which is an automatic, party-line vote for control of the House. But to this day I remember listening carefully as the name of each representative was called by the clerk and, eventually, I had to rise in the historic House chamber and call out the name of my party's candidate. One of my last votes as a member was on impeachment of the president, and I remember it too; it was hardly an auspicious way to end a voting career.

But voting is also a particularly difficult responsibility. This generally comes as a surprise to people. In the popular imagination, members of Congress don't have to work very hard to make voting decisions. They listen to their biggest campaign donors, or to powerful special interests, or to the polls, and then vote accordingly. Or perhaps they're captives of a particular ideology: Whatever the conservative or liberal line might be on a given bill, that's where they come down. As with many common perceptions about Congress, there's a germ of truth in all of this, but the reality is far more interesting.

Members recognize they are casting their votes to draft the basic laws of the nation, and they take this responsibility seriously. On average they participate in 95 percent of all votes held. They typically put a lot of effort into making sure they cast their votes in the most thoughtful and defensible way possible. They are well aware that they will frequently be called on in many different forums to defend how they voted.

Each vote has a different dynamic, and the approach members take in deciding how to cast it may vary, but in general the process includes several considerations:

First, as I've already suggested, members pay close attention to what they hear from their constituents and try to reflect the views of those who sent them to Washington. They get constituent letters, e-mails, faxes, and telephone calls by the hundreds or even thousands on some bills. Members also solicit constituent views through public meetings and questionnaires and stay on top of opinions back home by closely following local newspapers, media, and public opinion surveys. All too often, however, these constituent voices conflict with one another or are expressed in only the most general terms, so a member has to work hard to discern a majority sentiment.

Second, members get recommendations from a wide range of expert and political sources. They have stacks of background material sent by special-interest groups and think tanks; they can read page after page of testimony collected by congressional committees; colleagues in Congress send out letters with recommendations; the administration—and, on significant occasions, the president himself—will often weigh in as well. Members are aware of how their party's congressional leaders—as well as contributors to their campaigns—want them to vote on a particular issue. They also rely heavily on what like-minded colleagues or members with particular expertise think about an issue. It is quite common for members trying to make up their minds to seek the opinions of colleagues who are well respected for their issue expertise and have worked extensively in a particular area.

Third, members look beyond the recommendations to assess the major arguments being offered for or against a bill. The decisions can be difficult, since good points are often made on both sides of an issue. Members must sort through a host of arguments—legal, statistical, economic, moral, and pragmatic—and make a judgment as to which are most persuasive. After the vote is over and members have to explain their votes to constituents or to the media, they will almost always cite two or three of the main arguments or reasons they found most compelling.

Fourth, members bring their own core convictions and personal histories to the process. They don't come to Congress as blank slates, awaiting the directives of others. Instead, they may have strongly held core beliefs—such as the sanctity of life, the need for limited government, the imperative to help the less fortunate, or the importance of assisting a particular country or region of the world—that color their decisions on specific bills.

Deciding how to vote is complicated because it involves complicated issues. It is not as easy as the TV "sound bites" make it out to be. On some issues, members of Congress vote their consciences; on others, they follow what they think are the wishes of most of their constituents; on still others, particularly those votes that mean less to their own districts, they stick with their party leaders or some congressional faction, often in hopes of getting support later on a bill that matters more to them. Often, especially when the votes are coming quickly, they will take cues from respected like-minded colleagues. Sometimes, when a bill isn't of much consequence to particular members, they will respond to a colleague's plea on the floor: "I really need you on this one." Each bill that comes up involves a different calculation, but it always involves a calculation.

Imagine yourself in Congress, for instance, considering the Justice Department package of some forty changes to make it easier for law-enforcement officials to fight terrorism. Every day, your office staff has to deal with letters and calls from constituents urging you either to go along in the name of security or to proceed cautiously in the interest of safeguarding basic American liberties. Every day, you hear from a host of experts and interests from all sides of the issue advising you on the right course to take. An easy decision? Hardly. In the end, your vote will be black or white—you can only vote Yea or Nay—but casting it will have required a thorny analysis of shades of gray.

And this is just one issue. As a member of Congress, you cast hundreds of votes a year on everything from basic constitutional questions to cotton subsidies to tiny changes in a time zone. Moreover, sometimes you are faced with complex bills with hundreds of provisions, some of them good, some of them bad. Yet you must make a judgment on balance and cast one vote up or down. Though you may become well versed in many subjects taken up on the floor, you can't possibly get to know them all. And with all that is going on in Congress, finding the time to actually arrive at a decision can be a challenge. Yet on every single vote, you'll be expected to have an opinion and be able to defend it.

Members are intensely aware of the anguish their votes sometimes cause. A few years after I came to Congress, I offered one of the early amendments to reduce funding for our involvement in Vietnam, a move that put me squarely in opposition to the White House. We lost the vote, though we received more support than we had expected. I happened to go to the White House later that night. I'd been one of President Johnson's favorites from the House class of '64, and he had come to Indiana to campaign for me in 1966. He had taken a special interest in my career. I will never forget his eyes when he asked me, "How could you do that to me, Lee?"

The issues facing lawmakers when the time comes to vote are often complicated and numerous, and the recommendations and considerations can be varied. But in the end the final step is always the same. The member must make a decision and cast the vote, knowing that in our system of representative democracy he or she alone will be held accountable for that Yea or Nay.

The Frustrations and Rewards of Congress

I recently came across a letter from a well-known American politician to his wife. He was not impressed by the perks of his job. "The business of the Congress is tedious beyond expression," he complained. "Every man in it is a great man, an orator, a critic, a statesman; and therefore, every man, upon every question, must show his oratory, his criticism, and his political abilities."[6] Turn on C-SPAN any day that Congress is in session, and you'll see what that fellow meant.

What's interesting about this letter, though, is that its writer was John Adams, and he posted it to Abigail from Philadelphia in 1774, while the Continental Congress was in session. It's hard not to be taken aback by his dismay. This was, after all, an extraordinary collection of people bent on the extraordinary business of framing the charter of the new nation. Simply to be a part of it would have been exhilarating, you would think.

But then, some things have not changed in the 230 years since John Adams wrote that letter. In the popular mind, of course, being a member of Congress seems a glamorous and pampered job. There are the visits to the White House, the travel on Air Force planes, the big speeches, the media requests for statements on all sorts of issues, the sense of being at the center of big events and an initiate into the rituals of democracy. Being a member of Congress makes others pay attention.

Yet as a former congressman, what I remember just as strongly are the job's frustrations. Progress in a legislative body comes very slowly. You do things inch by inch, not mile by mile. A defeat on something you strongly believe in can be devastating. The hours are terribly long—made even longer by the fact that, when Congress is in session, you can never get away from the bells that tell you a vote is in progress and you have to drop whatever you're doing and run to the floor. This would be fine if the votes involved vital matters of state, but in a typical week you're asked to cast scores of inconsequential votes: procedural votes; votes that were brought up simply to please a tiny constituency; votes that are symbolic, not substantive; votes that the other party just wants to use to score political points.

Committee meetings go on without end, and the work itself is often tedious, requiring that you go over legislation comma by comma. You are constantly rushing from one meeting or appointment to another, and your daily schedule, meticulously worked out, is always being interrupted, revised, or simply scrapped. Constituent demands are unrelenting. If you have children, you're going to miss a good part of their lives, and with the constant travel, airports become as familiar as your home. You cannot plan ahead, whether for an evening off or for vacation, because some event or delay always demands that Congress stay in session longer than planned.

My wife can give you a long list of important family events I missed while I was in Congress, from church confirmations to honor society inductions (although I did make the graduations and the marriages). The first question I always ask someone telling me they want to run for Congress is: "How does your spouse feel about it?" Congress is tough on families. I came to Congress in 1965 with a very large freshman class; only a few of those marriages survived.

After a while, all the political posturing, sniping, and scrambles to claim credit for good things—or avoid blame for bad—become increasingly distressing, and the constant maneuvering for partisan advantage becomes ever more disheartening. And for putting up with all this, many members of Congress get paid less than they could make in the private sector and face harsh and frequent criticism.

Yet despite it all, most members run for reelection, many remain in office for decades, and there is always an enormous pool of talented people who want to serve in Congress. Why? Some like the trappings of power and the way the job feeds the ego; but most,

I think, are truly motivated by the belief that, hard as it is, they can make a difference in the lives of ordinary Americans.

Far from driving people out of politics, the give-and-take of public life is usually what most satisfies them. There is a pervasive sense on Capitol Hill that it is where the issues of greatest importance to the nation are being sorted out. Sometimes this is misplaced, but often it is not, because one of the things you quickly learn in office is that after two hundred years, we are still struggling over the questions that aroused the passions of this country's founding generation. How much power should the federal government be given? How far should government go in regulating our affairs or trying to better our lives? How do we resolve the tension between encouraging individual liberty and initiative and buttressing a central government strong enough to promote justice for all? John Adams, Thomas Jefferson, Alexander Hamilton, and James Madison tangled over these same questions. Our system's strength rests in part on the fact that these matters are subject to debate every time a new federal budget comes to a vote or a major presidential initiative gets introduced on Capitol Hill. When you arrive in Congress, you get a chance to take part in that ongoing debate and in our great experiment with democracy.

Quite simply, members feel the job is satisfying because they are contributing to the direction and the success of this country. They come from all parts of the country and all walks of life, at different stages of their careers, and they seem to disagree on just about everything. Yet almost all would say that by serving in Congress they can make a difference in the lives of people and in the affairs of the nation. They have a commitment to public service and they want to do good—to help their constituencies, their states, and their country as each of them sees fit. There is a certain camaraderie among them, even if they're ideological opponents, that stems from their engagement in the common pursuit of making this a better country. "I have a zeal in my heart, for my country and her friends, which I cannot smother or conceal," John Adams wrote his wife as he headed off to Philadelphia. I don't think that has changed in the 230 years since he wrote those words, either.

4

Public Criticisms of Congress

Many Americans might go along with my general explanation of how Congress works but still feel that it doesn't work particularly well. Public approval of how Congress is handling its job has typically been very low in recent decades, usually hovering around a 40 percent approval rating—sometimes going higher, sometimes falling below 30 percent.

I heard numerous criticisms of Congress while serving, often in fairly blunt terms. Many of the criticisms seemed to be quite perceptive; others were fairly far off the mark—such as when people thought that as a member of Congress I received a limousine and chauffeur, or enjoyed free medical care, or didn't pay Social Security or income taxes. Even though the attacks were sometimes unpleasant, I always felt it was important for constituents to relay their complaints about Congress, and I never took them lightly. When people are upset about Congress, it undermines public confidence in government and fosters cynicism and disengagement. In a representative democracy like ours, in which Congress must reflect the views and interests of the American people as it frames the basic laws of the land, it really does matter what people think about Congress.

This chapter will sort through several of the main public criticisms of Congress and how it works.

"Legislators Are a Bunch of Crooks"

Several years ago, I was watching the evening news on television when the anchorman announced the death of Wilbur Mills, the legendary former chairman of the House Ways and Means Committee. There was a lot he could have said. He might have recounted the central role Mills had played in creating Medicare. Or he might have talked about how Mills helped to shape the Social Security system and draft the tax code. But he didn't. Instead, he recalled how Mills's career had foundered after he had been found early one morning with an Argentinean stripper named Fanne Foxe. And then he moved on to the next story.

One of the perks of being chairman of an influential committee in Congress, as I was at the time, is that you can pick up the telephone and get through to television news anchors. Which I did: I chided him for summing up the man's career with a scandal. Much to my surprise, he apologized.

The fact is, though, he wasn't doing anything unusual. Americans of all stripes like to dwell on misbehavior by members of Congress. We look at the latest scandal and assume that we're seeing the *real* Congress. But we're not. People might hear repeatedly in the media about missteps, but they hear very little about the House leader who went home on weekends to pastor his local church, or the congressman who devoted decades to championing the needs of the elderly, or the senator who spent one day each month working in a local job to better understand the needs of constituents, or the many members who worked behind the scenes in a bipartisan way to reach the delicate compromises needed to make the system work.

Nor do I see members of Congress as basically out to enrich themselves at the public trough. During my time in office—when I heard numerous complaints about congressional "pay-grabs"—the salaries of members didn't even keep up with inflation. The pay I received in my last year in Congress was $20,000 *less* than if my 1965 pay had been adjusted for inflation. For most members, it is not the money that attracts them to public service; most could be making more in the private sector.

I don't want to claim that all members are saints and that their behavior is impeccable. Improper conduct does occur. Yet I agree with the assessment of historian David McCullough: "Congress, for all its faults, has not been the unbroken parade of clowns and thieves and posturing windbags so often portrayed. What should be spoken of more often, and more widely understood, are the great victories that have been won here, the decisions of courage and vision achieved."[1]

Probity in Congress is the rule rather than the exception, and most experts on Congress agree that it has gotten better over the years. A personal example: Back in the early 1970s, I made an argument in a committee hearing one day favoring military aid for one of our allies. When I got back to my office, I discovered a delegation from that country waiting for me; they wanted to thank me with a fat honorarium, a trip to their country, and an honorary degree from one of their universities. I declined.

The point here isn't my purity. It's that at the time this happened, there was nothing improper about their offer. Today, there would be. When I arrived in Congress, members could accept lavish gifts from special interests, pocket campaign contributions in their Capitol offices, and convert their campaign contributions to personal use. And they were rarely punished for personal corruption. None of that would be tolerated now.

Things still aren't perfect, and I'll return in the next chapter to the need for maintaining and enforcing tough standards of congressional ethics. But the ethical climate at the Capitol is well ahead of where it was a couple of decades ago. And, I might add, it is well ahead of the public perception. From my experience in Congress, getting to know hundreds of members of Congress well over the years, my clear impression is that the vast majority would whole-heartedly agree with Representative Barbara Jordan: "It is a privilege to serve people, a privilege that must be earned, and once earned, there is an obligation to do something good with it."[2]

"There's Too Much Wasteful, Pork-Barrel Spending by Congress"

Some years back, I was at a public meeting in Tell City, Indiana, when one of its citizens stood up to take me and my colleagues to task for our devotion to pork-barrel spending. How in good conscience, he wanted to know, could we spend so much of the public's money on frivolous projects designed only to get us reelected?

My first instinct was to ask him to step outside—but not in the way you might think. To understand why, you have to know a little about Tell City. It is a small town in southern Indiana, founded by Swiss settlers, not far from where Abraham Lincoln ran a ferry across the mouth of the Anderson River as a young man. What you notice in Tell City, though, is a much bigger river, the Ohio, which runs along the edge of its downtown. Indeed, between the building I was standing in and thousands of cubic feet of water lay only a few yards of ground and a levee. And the levee, as you've probably guessed, was built with federal money. If it weren't for this "pork-barrel" project, a good bit of Tell City would long since have been swept away. Pork, I told my audience, is in the eye of the beholder.

The vast majority of federal spending, I would argue, goes to important, widely supported uses. After all, more than half of total federal spending each year goes just for two things—national defense and seniors programs, both very popular. Yet I would agree that you can find some mighty debatable appropriations in each year's federal budget—$1.5 million aimed at refurbishing a statue in one powerful senator's state, $650,000 for ornamental fish research, $90,000 for the National Cowgirl Museum and Hall of Fame, and millions for various memorials and special projects that, in the scheme of things, will benefit relatively few Americans. Congress never fails to provide plenty of material for groups that make it their business to uncover questionable spending.

But think for a moment about what we characterize as "pork-barrel spending." Much of it is for infrastructure: highways, canals, reservoirs, dams, and the like. There's money for erosion-control projects, federal buildings, and military installations. There's support for museums and arts centers. There's backing for academic institutions, health-care facilities, and job-training institutes. All of these have some value and indeed may prove important to lots of people. When it comes to infrastructure spending, "pork-barrel projects" are rarely worthless. Members of Congress know in considerable detail the needs of their district or state, often better than the unelected federal bureaucrat who would otherwise decide where the money goes. We shouldn't fall into the trap of thinking that simply because a senator or representative directs the money to a specific project, it's waste, whereas if a bureaucrat or even the president does, it's not.

At the same time, my scolder in Tell City was on to something. While "pork" may provide valuable support to worthy projects, it can also shore up projects that most of the country would rightly question. The problem is, Congress often doesn't do a good job of distinguishing between the two.

To begin with, pork-barrel projects are frequently inserted by powerful members in spending bills surreptitiously, literally in the dark of night. It may happen within a day of the final vote on a spending measure, and most legislators don't even notice. Nothing is more frustrating for members than to vote for major national legislation only to discover later that it also contained obscure pork-barrel items like a Lawrence Welk memorial. And when legislators do notice a particular project and have concerns about it, they are often reluctant to object, because they may have legislation or projects of their own they don't want to put at risk.

The current process frequently doesn't allow Congress to weigh the relative merit of spending projects, to look at the interests of the country as a whole, or to weigh the needs of one region against another before deciding how to spend the public's money. The problem is not so much that the spending is wasted (it usually does some good) but whether it could better be spent for other projects. Congress often ignores this question and simply provides the money at the request of a member who is powerful or whose vote is badly needed.

We do need to recognize, as I discussed in chapter 2, that much of what Congress passes has an important impact on our lives. But we also need to focus more on wasteful spending, going after the bad apples that get all the attention. A few years ago when I was still in Congress, a reform committee I headed up recommended requiring that no bill could be voted on until all of the funding it earmarked for individual projects was listed clearly in publicly available reports. That would force proponents to justify publicly their provisions for special projects and would help ensure that fewer wasteful projects will pass. Sunshine is still the best disinfectant for wasteful proposals. And on that, I think my critic from Tell City and I could both agree.

"Legislators Just Bicker and Never Get Anything Done"

One of the most common criticisms of Congress is that members spend too much time arguing. I must have heard it a thousand times: Why can't you folks get together?

Congress is generally perceived as the "broken branch" of government, unable to work together to carry out the nation's wishes. Sometimes the language during debates gets a little rough, such as when a member in 1875 described another as "one who is outlawed in his own home from respectable society; whose name is synonymous with falsehood; who is the champion, and has been on all occasions, of fraud; who is the apologist of thieves; who is such a prodigy of vice and meanness that to describe him would sicken imagination and exhaust invective."[3] These comments make the recent partisan squabbling almost sound mild.

The perception of Congress as paralyzed by its own internal bickering comes up in most discussions of the institution, and it is one that matters. Surveys show it is a major factor in the American public's lack of confidence in Congress.

People get upset because they think that everyone agrees on what's right and necessary, and they can't understand why Congress doesn't simply implement the consensus. Yet the truth is that there is far less consensus in the country than is often thought. It is very difficult to get agreement among a broad cross-section of Americans on current major political issues. Most years there is little agreement on what the main issues are, let alone on what specific steps should be taken to address them. The devil—and the dispute—is often in the details.

Most bills passed by Congress actually receive fairly broad, bipartisan support. Yet dispute and delay often occur because it's a tough and tedious job making federal policy. The issues before Congress are much more numerous than in past years, often very complicated and technical, and intensely debated, with a large number of sophisticated groups knowing that key policies and millions of dollars can hinge on every word or comma. The great variety of our nation's races, religions, regional interests, and political philosophies all bring their often-conflicting views to Congress. It's the job of the House and Senate to hear all sides and to search for a broadly acceptable consensus.

There is bound to be bickering when you bring together 535 duly elected representatives and senators—all of whom feel strongly about issues, all of whom want to represent the best interests of their constituents. People shouldn't fall off their chairs because they see heated debate; that's how we thrash things out in a democratic society.

Much of what the public dislikes is part of the process. We could have chosen to have all decisions made by a single ruler at the top, but that's not the kind of government we wanted. Congress was set up as the forum in which strongly held differences would be aired; conflict is built into the system. Allowing all sides a chance to be heard on the most difficult issues facing our nation almost ensures that the debate will at times be contentious, but it also helps to keep our country from ripping apart.

Dispute is different from dysfunction, and results are what count. Intense debate doesn't mean that issues cannot be resolved. It's just that resolving them can be frustrating and time-consuming. I remember many conversations with disgruntled constituents over the years when I urged patience and suggested that they judge Congress by the final results, not by the bickering they might see during the process.

I'm not defending strongly partisan or harsh personal attacks. Certainly things can sometimes go too far and get out of hand. And Congress does have various means for handling such cases—the member in 1875 was in fact formally censured by the House for his remarks. But overall, people should expect some bickering and arguing within Congress. A democracy without conflict is not a democracy.

"You Can't Trust What Members of Congress Say"

I've been looking over some recent survey results on public attitudes toward members of Congress, and I'm worried. People generally give their representatives high marks for being informed about the issues and quite strong approval for their hard work. In fact, three out of four believe that most members of Congress work hard at their jobs. Yet there's an even higher proportion—almost 90 percent—who agree with the statement that most members of Congress will lie if they feel the truth might hurt them politically. That's a lot of Americans who don't trust their elected representatives.

What's interesting to me is that the level of trust *within* Congress—that is, among the senators and representatives who work together day in and day out—is far higher. That is because on Capitol Hill, trust is the coin of the realm; pretty much the worst thing that can happen to a member of Congress is to have word get around among your colleagues that you cannot be relied upon. In order to do their jobs, legislators have to work with others: They cut deals; they agree to support an ally on one issue in exchange for support on something more urgent to their own constituents; they rely on one another to move legislation forward or to block a bill they oppose. Members who renege on their commitments soon find it difficult, if not impossible, to achieve much of what they want—which may explain why I found the overwhelming majority of the hundreds of members of Congress I worked with to be fundamentally honest. I would be hard-pressed to come up with more than a few instances over thirty-four years when I thought fellow members lied to me.

Of course, my relationship with them was as legislator to legislator, not voter to politician. And the truth is, you can understand why there might be a wider gulf between the public and their representatives: Politicians make many speeches; they issue public statements; they give countless media interviews; they respond to letters and inquiries; they hold forums and meetings; they meet constituents in cafés and VFW halls. It's hardly surprising that in the course of this, they would sometimes be inconsistent or even contradictory. But I don't think a blanket criticism that you can't trust members of Congress is fair. So how does one explain it?

To begin with, I think part of the fault lies with members of Congress themselves. They are usually quite skillful with the use of language and parse their words carefully; after all, they want your support and do not want to antagonize you. A politician can often find a way to glide over his or her precise beliefs without actually lying. So it's crucial for members of the public to listen very carefully and ask hard follow-up questions if they find too much wiggle room in an answer.

But it's also true that what might appear to be an inconsistency or a lie is just the result of an honest politician struggling with the complexities of public policy as it moves through different stages of development. For one thing, the circumstances under which a legislator commits to a certain position often change. Think about national security, for instance: The answers our political leaders were giving to questions on security issues on September 10, 2001, were probably very different from the ones they have given since then. By the same token, legislation can take months, if not years, to work its way through the process, and quite often it looks very different at the end from how it started out. So a legislator may initially support a particular bill and tell his or her constituents, but eventually vote against it because amendments in committee or on the floor have made it unpalatable. Votes are, in the end, a blunt instrument: They're yes or no, up or down, and they simply cannot reflect all the nuances of a member's thinking or the changes and complexity of the issues.

It's important to keep this in mind, because on any given issue, a legislator's opinions are usually quite complex, formed through conversations with lobbyists, other legislators, constituents, experts in the field, and others. It is often hard to convey all the nuances, conditions, and qualifications that make up one's position, and even if a politician does so, voters often forget them. Certainly, I've had the experience of a constituent assuring me that I said such-and-such a year ago, when I knew quite well that what I had said was more qualified than that.

I don't want to say that members of Congress never lie. But they do try to be careful with their public statements. They realize that there are a lot of people out there—political opponents, watchdog groups, reporters—who might like to catch them lying or making inconsistent statements. As former Illinois senator Everett Dirksen, known for his flowery oratory, would say, "I must use beautiful words. . . . I never know when I'll have to eat them."[4]

Perhaps Americans' cynicism about their representatives' truthfulness is just part and parcel of living in an age when public service as a whole is looked upon skeptically. Perhaps it's just a broad-brush criticism of Congress, without much to back it up, and people for the most part trust their own particular representative; certainly, the high rate at which members of Congress win reelection suggests they enjoy the support of their constituents. But even if it's simply the institution as a whole that suffers from such extensive distrust, it's a serious problem for representative democracy. And all of us—politicians and voters alike—need to work harder at improving the public dialogue.

"Congress Almost Seems Designed to Promote Total Gridlock"

People will often complain about a "do-nothing" Congress and think much of the fault lies in the basic design of Congress. When a single senator can hold up action on a popular measure, when thirty committees or subcommittees are all reviewing the same bill, when a proposal needs to move not just through both the House and Senate but also through their multilayered budget, authorization, and appropriations processes, when floor procedures are so complex that even members serving several years can still be confused by them—how can you expect to get anything done?

This feeling is magnified by the major changes American society has undergone in recent decades. The incredible increase in the speed of every facet of our lives from communication to transportation, has made many people feel that the slow, untidy, deliberate pace of Congress is not up to the demands of modern society.

It is not now, nor has it ever been, easy to pass legislation through Congress. But there is actually a method to the madness, and basic roadblocks were put into the process for a reason. We live in a great big complicated country, with enormous regional, ethnic, and economic diversity; it is, quite simply, a difficult country to govern. Moving slowly is required for responsiveness and deliberation.

The quest for consensus within Congress can be painfully slow. Issues involving spending and taxes, health care, and access to guns and abortion stir strong emotions and don't submit easily to compromise. Inside-the-Beltway scuffling annoys many Americans, but think about it: Do we really want a speedy system in which laws would be pushed through before a consensus develops? Do we really want a system in which the viewpoint of the minority gets trampled by a rush to action by the majority? Certainly reforms can be made to improve the system, but the basic process of careful deliberation, negotiation, and compromise lies at the very heart of representative democracy. Ours is not a parliamentary system; the dawdling pace comes with the territory.

We misunderstand Congress's role if we demand that it be a model of efficiency and quick action. Our country's founders never intended it to be. They clearly understood that one of the key roles of Congress is to slow down the process—to allow tempers to cool and to encourage careful deliberation, so that unwise or damaging laws do not pass in the heat of the moment and so that the views of those in the minority get a fair hearing. That basic vision still seems wise today. Proceeding carefully to develop consensus is arduous and exasperating, but it's the only way to produce policies that reflect the varied perspectives of a remarkably diverse citizenry. People may complain about the process, yet they also benefit from its legislative speed bumps when they want their views heard, their interests protected, their rights safeguarded. As Sam Rayburn used to say: "One of the wisest things ever said was, 'Wait a minute.'"

I'll return to this topic in the next chapter, discussing what sorts of reforms could make Congress work better. I certainly recognize that sometimes there are too many roadblocks in the system and Congress needlessly gets bogged down. Some streamlining and institutional reform is often needed, and I've been involved in many of those reform efforts. Yet I still believe that the fundamental notion that the structure of Congress should contain roadblocks and barriers to hasty action and unfair action makes sense for our country and needs to be protected and preserved.

"Members of Congress Compromise Too Much"

Every two years while I served in Congress, almost like clockwork, I'd open my mail to find the questionnaire. When you run for office, you expect various organizations to examine your positions on the issues they care about, but the group that sent this one out always went to greater lengths than most. For page after page, they'd ask me yes or no questions about matters large and small. There was no room for shades of gray; in their eyes, policy decisions were a matter of black or white.

I always felt boxed into a corner by this, even though I sympathized with their effort to publicize candidates' positions. If you take a larger view of the legislative process, they were doing themselves—and the rest of us—a disservice. At its best, politics is not a matter of holding onto your opinions no matter what; it's the art of finding common ground with people who think differently, then forging a workable approach to resolving a problem. This usually involves a compromise. Groups interested only in locking legislators into a rigid position make it more difficult for our democracy to work.

To be sure, many Americans don't understand this. Surveys show that three out of five believe that "compromise" means selling out one's principles and that members of Congress compromise too much. But think for a moment about what this means. What are the options when you can't forge a compromise? If the forces interested in the matter are equally strong, you get an impasse: Nothing happens. If they're not evenly matched, you get a triumphant majority and a deeply unhappy minority—a situation our nation's founders repeatedly warned against. And in the worst case, which our nation experienced when it came to the institution of slavery, you get a civil war.

At the end of the day, the responsibility of our politicians is to make the country work, to provide stability and an environment in which Americans can live in freedom and achieve their goals. In a nation as big and diverse as ours, in which so many people hold so many differing opinions, that means finding solutions to issues that allow us to work peaceably and productively together; and that, in turn, means finding compromises. It is what our founders did when they wrote the Constitution—they compromised on everything, from how small and large states would be represented to their deferment of the issue of slavery—and it is what virtually every piece of major legislation passed by Congress has required. As former House Speaker Joseph Cannon often said, "Nearly all legislation is the result of compromise."[5]

There are, of course, members of Congress who promise in their election campaigns to "fight for" their constituents, or for a particular cause, without backing down. But they usually discover that it is very difficult to be effective in Congress unless they learn how to build consensus. For the bottom line is, you cannot pass legislation unless you can get 218 members of the House of Representatives and 51 members of the Senate (frequently more) to agree with you. Members who don't learn the art of compromise usually find themselves on the margins of the legislative process. At the same time, every member of Congress has certain core beliefs on which he or she will not compromise; as much as finding common ground is part of the art of legislating, so, too, is weighing whether or not one is giving up too much in order to move an issue forward. Legislators make tough calls like that every day.

I don't wish to diminish those legislators who are deeply committed to an issue and choose to stick to it even at the risk of appearing to be a gadfly. They too serve our democracy, because these sometimes lone voices may, over time, change the agenda, shift the emphasis on an issue, or influence the nature of the resulting compromise. But if all legislators shunned consensus in favor of single-minded devotion to a cause, nothing would get done.

It has grown more difficult in recent years to practice the politics of consensus. This is due partly to the rising partisanship that has marked Congress over the past dozen years or so, partly to a press corps that always wants an immediate response and is ready to pounce on any instance of "inconsistency" in a politician's position, partly to the openness with which much of the legislative process operates these days, and partly to voters and interest groups who demand "purity" in a legislator's positions. Don't get me wrong: I think much good has come out of opening committees and other venues for deliberation to allow the public to see their representatives in action, and I supported many congressional "sunshine" reforms over the years. But I also think that legislators need room to act like politicians, to search for broadly acceptable solutions to difficult problems.

For one of the keenest insights our founders possessed was that the process by which we arrive at decisions matters a great deal. Legislating is not like war, in which one side strives to impose its will on the other. It is, rather, a shared path, the route we all must follow as we try to live with one another and struggle together to resolve the difficult questions that always confront us. We want our legislators to be able to work together, to give some ground when they need to in order to move forward. "If every compromise is taken as a defeat that must be overturned," wrote the eminent American historian Bernard Bailyn not long ago, "and if no healing generosity is shown to defeated rivals, the best-contrived constitution in the world would not succeed."[6] A willingness to compromise is nothing more or less than the recognition that we're all in this together for the long haul and that each of us has a stake in the system by which we govern ourselves.

"There's Too Much Money in Politics Today"

People hear the stories about all the fund-raising that members must do today, and so they believe that Congress is a "bought" institution. Often they would tell me that in our system dollars speak louder than words and that access is bought and sold. By a four-to-one margin, Americans believe that elected officials are influenced more by pressures from campaign contributors than by what is in the best interests of the country.

The problem of money in politics has been with us for many years. But it has really emerged as a serious problem in recent decades with the advent of television advertising. The biggest portion of my $1 million campaign budget—for a largely rural seat in southern Indiana—went for television.

Having experienced it firsthand, it is clear to me that the "money chase" has gotten out of hand. A lot of money from special interests is floating around Capitol Hill—in fact, far too much money. I believe it's a problem we ignore at our own peril.

To be fair, many of the claims of special interests buying influence in Congress are overstated. I would be the last to say that contributions have no impact on a member's voting record. But it should also be kept in mind that most of the money comes from groups who already share your views on the issues and want to see you reelected, rather than from groups who are hoping to change your mind. In addition, many influences shape members' voting decisions—including their assessment of the arguments, the opinions of experts and colleagues, their party's position, and, most importantly, what their constituents want. In the end, members know that if their votes aren't in line with what their constituents want, they simply won't be reelected. And that, rather than a campaign contribution, is what is foremost in their minds.

Yet it is still an unusual member of Congress who can take thousands of dollars from a particular group and not be affected by it at all. I have come to the view that the influence of money on the political process raises a threat to representative democracy. But more on that in the next chapter. Overall, this is an area in which I agree that significant reform is needed. It is also, unfortunately, an area in which there are no easy answers.

"Members Are Out of Touch with Their Constituents"

It always makes me wince when I hear someone criticize Congress as "out of touch" with what the people are thinking. I heard this complaint regularly when I was in Congress. Polls consistently show that more than 60 percent of the public do not expect their elected officials to be responsive to their thoughts.

This is a long-standing problem. Some of America's most animated political debates over the years have focused on whether the federal government is in close enough touch with the concerns of the average citizen. The framers of the Constitution fought at length on this point. One faction, led by Virginia's George Mason, called for many seats in the House of Representatives, so each district would be small enough for "common men" to personally communicate their concerns to House members. They were opposed by the Federalists, who argued that if each member represented more people, the House would more likely act in the national interest.

Under our system of representative democracy, members of Congress are asked not just to pass the nation's laws but also to represent in Washington the interests of the districts and states they represent. This means that staying in touch with constituents remains a fundamental challenge. It isn't a problem that will soon be going away.

I know how difficult it is for members of Congress to keep in touch with their huge constituencies. Some congressional districts are geographically vast—a single House member, for example, represents all of Alaska—and the population of each of our 435 House districts now averages 650,000 people, a number the founders could scarcely have imagined. When the first Congress convened in 1789, each of its sixty-five House members represented around 30,000 people. Our congressional constituencies today are the largest in the world, except for those in India.

The way Congress was set up, the House is assigned primary responsibility for understanding and voicing the concerns of the people. That's why the Constitution mandates House elections every two years. If the House fails in its job as chief citizen-advocate, then the people's faith in the federal government is eroded.

Contrary to the public perception, most legislators try very hard to keep in touch. They understand their weighty responsibility and think about this all the time. It is a constant topic of conversation among members over lunch or as they walk together between meetings—always comparing techniques, always trying to find ways to improve their outreach to constituents.

Indeed, I think a case could be made that the opposite may in fact be closer to the truth—that members today might be paying *too much* attention to every blip in the public opinion polls, thinking *too much* about what would play well back in the district, rather than focusing on what would be good policy and good for the country. So a balance is needed.

Members employ a wide variety of methods to reach out to constituents—traditional ones like sending out newsletters, hosting local forums, encouraging office visits, participating in radio and television call-in shows, and attending civic functions and community festivals, as well as using the latest technology for satellite hookups, video conferencing, and "virtual town meetings" over the Internet. They make sure that constituents who write, e-mail, fax, or contact their congressman get a letter in response.

Because House districts now are so populous, even a frenetic pace allows a member to reach only a small portion of his or her constituency. And yet members keep trying to push the envelope on public contact, particularly when they are back home. They do this because handshaking at the county fair and Fourth of July parades and other such gatherings is often the only way to have any contact with constituents who are indifferent to politics or are simply too busy in their everyday lives to bother to write or call their congressman.

Most members of Congress feel a deep sense of obligation to reach out to the public. It is an ongoing challenge for them, and they recognize they simply need to keep working at it.

Legislators have been struggling at this for more than two hundred years without resolving it. Citizens, too, need to understand their obligation to make our democratic system function well. They have some responsibility to help their representative *not* get out of touch by initiating contacts and responding when they can to members' outreach efforts. It takes the participation and goodwill of all to make our system work.

"Congress Is Run by Lobbyists and Special Interests"

Americans have different views of lobbyists and special interests. Some see them as playing an essential part in the democratic process. Others look at them with some skepticism, but understand that they have a role to play in developing policy. Yet most see them as sinister forces with too much control of Congress. The recent Enron and Arthur Andersen scandals, and revelations about those companies' extensive lobbying of Congress, have fed this cynicism about the hold that powerful private interests maintain over public policy. Americans continue to remain suspicious that Congress is manipulated by powerful wheeler-dealers who put enormous pressure on legislators or buy votes through extensive campaign contributions and other favors. It is not an unfounded concern, and it is not going to go away, no matter how fervently some might try to dismiss it.

Now, the popular view of lobbyists as nefarious fat cats smoking big cigars and handing out $100 bills behind closed doors is wrong. These days, lobbyists are usually principled people who recognize that their word is their bond. They are aggressive in seeking out members of Congress, offering to take them to dinner for a chance at a longer conversation, and operating from a carefully worked-out game plan that takes into account who might be persuaded to vote their way, when they ought to be approached, and whether they have interested constituents who can be used effectively to put pressure on them. Lobbying is an enormous industry today with billions of dollars riding on its outcomes. Special interest groups will often spend millions of dollars on campaigns to influence a particular decision—through political contributions, grassroots lobbying efforts, television advocacy ads, and the like—because they know they can get a lot more back than they spent. Lobbyists who can get the kind of language they want into a bill can reap very large rewards. They are very good at what they do, and members of Congress can sometimes be easily swayed by them.

The influence of lobbyists on the process is not as simple as it might appear. In the first place, "special interests" are not just the bad guys. If you're retired, or a homeowner, or use public transit, or fly on airplanes, or are concerned about religious freedom, there are people in Washington lobbying on your behalf. With an estimated 25,000 interest groups lobbying in Washington, you can be sure your views are represented in many ways. Advocacy groups help Congress understand how legislation affects their members, and they help focus the public's attention on important issues. They play a vital role in amplifying the flow of information that Thomas Jefferson called the "dialogue of democracy."

In addition, Congress often takes up controversial, attention-grabbing issues on which you'll find an entire spectrum of opinions. Public notice is high, a host of special interests are weighing in, and lobbyists as well as legislators themselves are all over the map. In these circumstances, the prospect is very small that any single interest group or lobbyist can disproportionately influence the results. Quite simply, there are too many of them involved for that to happen, and the process is too public.

Where you have to look out is when things get quiet, when measures come up that are out of the public eye. A small change in wording here, an innocuous line in a tax bill there—that's where specific groups can reap enormous benefits that might not have been granted had they been held up to close public scrutiny.

The answer, it seems to me, is not to decry lobbying or lobbyists. In our system of government, we make a lot of trade-offs, as James Madison warned more than two centuries ago when he argued that "factions" were part of the cost of maintaining a democracy. At heart, lobbying is simply people banding together to advance their interests, whether they are farmers or environmentalists or bankers. Belonging to an interest group—the Sierra Club, the AARP, the Chamber of Commerce—is one of the main ways Americans participate in public life these days.

When I was in Congress, I found that organized groups not only brought a useful perspective to the table. They also pointed out how a given measure might affect my constituents in ways I hadn't considered. Lobbyists are typically professionals with a variety of skills: They are experts in their subject, with a sophisticated knowledge of the political process and the ability to raise large sums of money and make campaign contributions. They maintain extensive contacts, can generate grassroots support, and often have experience in putting together winning coalitions. I came to think of lobbyists as an important part of the *public discussion* of policy.

I emphasize "public discussion" for a reason. Sunshine is a powerful disinfectant, and rather than trying to clamp down on lobbying, I believe we would be better off ensuring that it happens in the open and is part of the broader policy debate.

So our challenge is not to shut it down but to make sure it's a balanced dialogue and that those in power don't consistently listen to the voices of the wealthy and the powerful more intently than to others. Several legislative proposals have been made over the years that would help, including campaign finance reform, strict limits on gifts to members of Congress, travel restrictions for members and their staffs funded by groups with a direct interest in legislation, and effective disclosure of the role lobbyists play in drafting legislation. But in the end, something may be even more important: ongoing conversation between elected officials and the people they represent.

Under our system of government, there is absolutely nothing wrong with lobbyists advocating their point of view. Lobbying is a key element of the legislative process and part of the free speech guaranteed under our Constitution. Members of Congress, I would argue, have a responsibility to listen to lobbyists. But members also have a responsibility to understand where these lobbyists are coming from, to sort through what they are saying, and then to make a judgment about what is in the best interests of their constituents and the nation as a whole.

Conclusion

Members of Congress most often will hear from constituents on specific policy issues—how the legislator should vote, issues that need more attention, local problems that aren't being addressed. But equally important is hearing complaints about how Congress as an institution is working. If people are upset that members seem increasingly dishonest or out of touch, that special interests seem to be taking over, or that there is too much partisan bickering or legislative gridlock or whatever—all of these are important things for members of Congress to hear.

Such feedback is essential for keeping Congress on course. It's how Congress adjusts itself when it gets off track—hearing from all corners that something is just not right and then trying to be responsive. Making Congress work better is not just a matter for the political scientists or the political commentators or the legislators themselves. Congress really is the people's branch, and we all have the responsibility to keep an eye on it and to speak up when we're bothered by what we see. It's an essential part of the ongoing dialogue of democracy.

5

Key Ways Congress Could Work Better

AMERICANS CLEARLY HAVE DEEP CONCERNS about Congress, but they wouldn't want to abandon their long-established form of government. In all the years I was in Congress, although my constituents were not at all hesitant about bashing Congress, they still thought it important for it to be around.

There is, in short, strong support for the institution of the Congress—for its role in the balance of powers, for its role in giving a voice to the people, for its role as a forum for resolving national differences—but also deep frustration with its operations and day-to-day functioning, a frustration, I might add, often shared by many members.

So how do we make Congress work better—restoring greater confidence in its operations and making it a more effective, less frustrating body? Given the way it was set up under the Constitution, with numerous checks and balances and multiple layers to allow all voices a chance to be heard, Congress will never be a model of efficiency. Yet important improvements can still be made. This chapter contains several basic changes that I believe are central to the proper functioning of Congress. Rather than presenting a long list of technical changes in the legislative and budget processes, I've focused on broader, more fundamental improvements, a few suggestions from the perspective of someone who has spent more than three decades immersed in this fascinating, complex institution.

Declining Civility

Not long ago I was asked to give a talk on how Congress has changed since 1965, the year I entered it as a young freshman member from southern Indiana. As I sat looking through my old speeches, a phrase jumped out at me. Congress, I told my audiences back then, did its work in an "extraordinarily hospitable atmosphere." Indeed, I liked to say, no matter how spirited the policy debate, "a cocoon of warmth" surrounded us.

If I suggested anything of the sort today I'd be laughed out of the room. The last several years have been particularly divisive and partisan. Certainly tough times in Congress are nothing new—going back even to the Second Congress, in 1791, when partisan differences undermined its ability to function, and including the memorable floor debate in the 1850s when thirty members pulled their guns. Yet, during my time in Congress, I witnessed a marked change in its atmosphere: the demonization of people in the other party, nasty personal attacks, a willingness to pull out all the stops to undermine the other side's agenda, and concerted efforts to topple the other party's leader.

Breakdowns in civility are among the most serious threats to the ability of Congress to work well. Spirited, even heated debates and aggressively pushing the interests of your constituents are to be expected and are healthy to the institution. That's how issues get thrashed out in a democratic society. But personal attacks and excessive partisanship poison the atmosphere of Congress and undermine the ability of members to come together to do the nation's business. It even got so bad in the 1990s that Representative John

Myers, a Republican colleague from Indiana, and I requested a report from the Congressional Research Service on the rules and precedents governing civility and decorum in the House and circulated it to all of our colleagues.

Yet the situation isn't hopeless. Some periods are distressing, yet others do give reason for hope. In 1995, one of my last years in Congress, there was a stark ideological divide between Democrats and the Republican majority. Debates were contentious and bitterly uncompromising; legislators almost came to blows on a few occasions. As the country watched with increasing disapproval, the congressional leadership that winter shut down much of the federal government for twenty-seven days, a move that caused Congress's standing with the public to plummet.

Then something important happened. Just before the traditional August break in 1996, Congress turned itself around. In the space of just ten days, Democrats and Republicans came together and passed several major bills—overhauling the federal welfare program, expanding access to health insurance, increasing the minimum wage, and rewriting safe drinking water legislation. Congress showed very quickly and very clearly that even when it appears ready to sink, it can right itself. Faced with the prospect of returning to their districts not only empty-handed but widely reviled for their obstinate partisanship, members of Congress rediscovered pragmatism. They sat down together and wrote laws.

Congress is a partisan body, but it is also a responsive body. When constituents are tired of division and blatant partisan calculation, members of Congress hear about it when they go home, and they change course. The surprise would be if members *did not* pay attention. It is Congress's own self-correcting mechanism at work.

I don't want to overstate the point. The basic forces that over the years have produced this partisan era are not simply going to fade away: the rise of personal attack campaigns and their frequent success, the intense pressure on members' time that leaves little opportunity to develop friendships across the aisle, the hard-fought battle for control of Congress every two years, the many noncompetitive elections that have allowed members to appeal to their partisan bases rather than move toward the center, the desire of the media to highlight the extremes, and the generally less civil tone in society at large. As Congress moves into substantive debates—over the budget, the fate of Social Security, tax cuts, national security policy—vigorous partisanship will no doubt prevail. Some of it will be "good" partisanship—tough debate over the merits of the issues; that's the role that partisanship ought to play in a representative government. Some of it may still get out of hand.

Yet the basic point is that the American people can have a significant impact on how Congress behaves. Politicians may be tough advocates for strongly held positions, but they do respond when the public demands that they cooperate with opponents to try to resolve differences and reach consensus.

Back in the days of that "warm cocoon," when I was still learning my way around Congress, I made a mistake on the House floor. I was managing a bill for the Democrats, and I forgot a small parliamentary move that would have locked victory in place. William Bray, a prominent Republican who was also from Indiana, came over to me, put his arm on my shoulder, gently pointed out my blunder, and showed me how to fix it. And this was on a bill he *opposed*. That was how Congress worked then. We're a long way from that atmosphere on Capitol Hill today, and, quite frankly, it's not at all clear at this point which direction Congress will go in the years ahead. But I'd like to think that, as Congress tries to address our nation's important challenges, its members are beginning once again to discover how much more they can accomplish by working together.

The Importance of Good Process

When I was in Congress, I must have served on just about every congressional panel that sought to improve the institution's structure and operations, from the Bolling Committee on Committees and Obey Administrative Review Commission in the

1970s to later cochairing the Joint Committee on the Organization of Congress in the 1990s. Attentive constituents would sometimes ask me about this, since few people can imagine anything more tedious than the details of the legislative process. Why, they wondered, would I choose to spend time considering such arcane matters as motions to recommit, or cloture votes, or the number of subcommittees? I have to confess, there were some mind-numbing moments when I had to ask myself the same question. Yet in the end I always felt it was worth it. To me, Congress can't function properly without good process. And in too many cases, we're losing it.

Most Americans are familiar with the standard textbook diagrams of how a bill becomes law, with one step following neatly after another. The truth is, astute legislators can get around virtually any step in the process. And members of Congress are increasingly choosing to pursue this "unconventional lawmaking," as it is sometimes politely called, when it comes to important legislation—the kind of legislation, in other words, that deserves full scrutiny, not back-door maneuvering.

For example, a proposal might bypass the important committee review process—that's where the hard questions tend to get asked—if a member of Congress can convince the leadership to tack it onto another bill that has already cleared the committee. Even a committee chairman might discover bills his committee had approved heading to the floor with provisions he's never seen before (something I found particularly unsettling as a chairman). Or, as is happening more frequently in the House, a bill might be brought to the floor under restrictive rules that permit few or no amendments, essentially cutting off most legislators' chances to improve legislation.

One of the most pernicious developments of recent decades has been the habit of assembling so-called "omnibus" bills—these are measures that contain literally thousands of provisions, many of them unrelated—and then attaching them to legislation that must pass to prevent the federal government from shutting down. In a recent Congress, for example, a single omnibus bill contained major changes in Medicare, banking, farm programs, welfare, veterans assistance, student loans, environmental preservation, small business support, and hundreds of other issues. Almost every key policy change of that session was put into this single bill. In 2003, the omnibus funding bill weighed thirty-two pounds, was over three thousand pages in length, and contained eleven of the thirteen appropriations bills that should have been considered and passed separately.

Such omnibus bills—which have been routinely used under the leadership of both parties—might be put together by leadership staff, sometimes with the help of outside lobbyists, and presented to legislators at 3:00 A.M. with a vote scheduled just a few hours later; usually that vote can only be Yea or Nay, with no chance for amendments. So in addition to making it nearly impossible for members of Congress to read and understand the bill before they vote on it, the procedure keeps them from trying to remove its more obnoxious provisions should they happen to discover one.

Less than half the bills that become law these days go through all the stages of the standard legislative process—sometimes because the measure has already been thoroughly aired, and sometimes because members want to avoid roadblocks or too much scrutiny. The leadership and members of both parties have become extremely skillful over the last several years at manipulating the rules and circumventing the regular order to get the results they want. For them, the end clearly justifies the means.

Good process boils down to fairness. It is amazing how often members in positions of power will acknowledge that the process they control is not fair but is, in their view, necessary to get the bill passed. One wonders about the harm this does to the system.

So it's worth taking a step back and asking whether there is a cost to bypassing good procedure. Is quickly moving a desired piece of legislation the only goal? Certainly our country's founders didn't think so. They designed a system in which all new proposals get careful scrutiny by going through many layers of review. They were far less interested in moving good ideas efficiently than they were in preventing bad ideas from passing in the heat of the moment and becoming the law of the land. Granted, an extraordinary procedure might sometimes be needed. Yet the founders would be appalled at how often these days the process is circumvented to advance ideas that would have virtually no chance if considered carefully on their own.

The truth is, traditional lawmaking is not just a nicety—it's a necessity if we are to remain a democracy. The careful review of new ideas is the only way all viewpoints and interests can be heard. It is what allows the majority to rule without sacrificing respect for those in the minority or cutting off access to the system for those without an "in" with the leadership. When this process is abridged, we lose the transparency, accountability, openness, and accessibility that are fundamental to the system's fairness. We need to make sure we do not abandon the careful, thorough deliberation our country's founders had in mind, for in the end, democracy is a process, not a product.

Better White House/Congress Consultation

One of the most dominant features of American government in recent years has been the way the voters have chosen a president from one party and a Congress under the control of the other. In recent times this has been the rule rather than the exception, as some two-thirds of the elections since 1952 have produced divided government. That complicates an already complicated relationship between Congress and the president.

Under our system of balanced and shared powers, the president and Congress need to find ways to come together to get about the business of running the country. The president today largely sets the broad national agenda. But the simple truth is, he cannot run the country alone. To make a record for his administration, he has no choice but to find points of accord with Congress. Yet Congress was designed not to automatically go along with what's on the president's agenda but to check and counterbalance a strong executive. Each is wary of ceding too much power to the other, and with every significant issue scrutinized for its impact on the next election, we shouldn't expect a paradise of cooperation. To help ensure that better policy emerges, a basic and fundamental tension between Congress and the president is built into the system, making this one of the enduring conflicts in our government.

This relationship has seen some tough times in recent years. During my first few years in the House, Congress agreed with President Lyndon Johnson's positions on legislation more than 80 percent of the time. In my last few years, Congress's support of President Clinton's policies was closer to 50 percent. One factor is whether the president is skillful in his dealings with Congress, as, for example, Johnson was initially, as a result of his years as Senate minority and majority leader. Another is the level of support for the president's policies that Congress perceives among the American people. But perhaps most important is whether Congress and the president have similar ideological views. Sometimes that's the case, but often it is not.

As our most representative branch, Congress articulates the concerns of many segments of the population. So a president who finds a way of forging consensus in Congress by knitting together contrasting views is also a president whose policies have a good chance of generating strong public support.

How does he develop a working relationship with Congress? To begin with, he has to have a very clear idea of what he wants. Congress is a morass these days, pulled in many directions by talented lobbyists of all stripes and by an astoundingly diverse and vocal population. If the president doesn't lay out a clear and realistic agenda and then stick to it, he'll be buffeted every which way.

Yet to make progress on his agenda, he must make a real effort to consult with Congress. I don't mean the sham sort of consultation in which the president calls congressional leaders in, or sends executive branch officials up to Capitol Hill, and says, "Here is our policy; there's no alternative." Real consultation takes work and a recognition that there are always alternatives in policy disputes. It means that Congress and the White House must sit down and talk before decisions are made. It means holding conversations among leaders—congressional leaders of both parties, the president, and his top advisors. And it means a commitment to sustaining the conversation beyond the crisis of the moment; after all, an administration that builds ties in calm periods will have a rapport with members of Congress when the next crisis develops. Generally, I felt that most of the administrations I served with did an inadequate job of consulting with Congress.

Congress too has in many ways fallen short. It needs to make consultation a higher institutional priority and streamline its operations to remove unnecessary roadblocks to developing consensus. More basically, Congress needs to work to have a serious discussion rather than score political points. Both branches must understand their proper constitutional roles and engage in a genuine dialogue on the problems that concern them most.[1]

Back in 1993, I joined several House colleagues to introduce a bill establishing a working group made up of the congressional leadership and leaders of the main committees involved in foreign policy to consult regularly with the president and his key national security advisors. The group would meet once a month, with other legislators with specific interests joining the group's work on certain issues. Having such a group would allow the executive to consult with a wide range of congressional leaders in a single setting. And it would provide a centralized forum for regular policy discussions on a wide range of issues, fostering mutual trust between the two branches. Our effort failed, but it's the kind of thing that would help and could be expanded to other areas.

Consultation does not—and should not—ensure agreement between the president and Congress. Differences will often remain, especially on the toughest issues. Congress has a responsibility to challenge administration proposals with which it disagrees. But even on those issues, consultation helps smooth some of the hard edges of disagreement, and it almost always refines and strengthens policy.

Over the years I've learned to be patient with democracy. I've learned that representative government works if you give it time.

There is a great temptation, particularly for new presidents, to try to get too much done too soon. They need to trust the system. The Constitution gives members of Congress the right to deliberate, and they properly exercise that right. It may not be the most efficient form of government, but it is the freest.

True Congressional Oversight

Whenever there is a juicy headline about a possible presidential misdeed or some apparent agency blunder, some member of Congress—most likely from the opposing party—will inevitably demand "oversight" hearings.

Depending on your politics, you might see this as an unwarranted partisan attack or a heartening sign that our elected representatives still know how to watch over the activities of the executive branch and rein in its excesses. I see it differently. I think it is a reminder of the need for Congress to improve its oversight substantially—to make it more balanced, wide-ranging, and in-depth.

Don't get me wrong. Misconduct and scandals certainly occur. Ever since its first inquiry in 1792—looking into government conduct of the wars against the Indians—Congress has played a crucial role in checking the abuse of executive powers. It did this in the Teapot Dome scandal of 1923, and again in the cases of Watergate and Iran-Contra, which took a significant amount of my time in the late 1980s. Although oversight is an implied rather than enumerated power for Congress in the Constitution, it has a rich history. Over the years, members of Congress have unearthed many policy failures, saved taxpayers billions of dollars, and identified corrupt or illegal behavior by executive branch officials.

But in recent years, congressional "oversight" has increasingly come to mean a focus on personal investigations, possible scandals, and issues that are designed to generate media attention. Congress has lost sight of the importance of traditional oversight.

This is a problem because good oversight stands at the core of good government. It is Congress's way of making sure that the administration is carrying out federal law in the way Congress intended. Passing legislation and providing oversight are two key functions of Congress, but almost all the attention goes to legislating. I agree with Woodrow Wilson, who said, "Quite as important as lawmaking is vigilant oversight of administration."[2]

Good oversight helps Congress evaluate how programs are administered and how they perform—ferreting out waste and fraud, determining whether programs have outlived their usefulness, compelling the administration to explain or justify its policies. It means reviewing how our food and workplace safety laws are working, checking the effectiveness of foreign aid programs, gauging the impact of clean water and clean air legislation, and looking for unneeded overlap in weapons systems. It is often tedious, technical, unglamorous work. But when done well, it can display the activities of government to ordinary citizens, protect the country from bureaucratic arrogance, and expose and prevent misconduct.

The responsibility of oversight is to look into every nook and cranny of governmental affairs—exposing what the government does, or does not do, and putting the light of publicity to it. And the tools of Congress are many. When I chaired the Foreign Affairs Committee, we emphasized not just regular oversight hearings but also closed briefings, on-site visits, written statements for the record, informal contacts, and GAO investigations. In many ways, Congress underestimates its power in oversight. Federal departments and agencies get a little nervous whenever someone from Congress starts poking around, and that is probably to the good.

But in recent times, the oversight priorities of Congress have generally shifted away from the careful review of programs to highly adversarial attempts at discrediting individual public officials, looking at length into Hillary Clinton's commodity transactions or probing deeply into the private lives of presidential nominees Clarence Thomas and John Tower. These personal investigations, while sometimes necessary, have been used excessively, consuming executive branch time and resources and, more importantly, diverting congressional time and resources from the more constructive work of policy oversight. Even worse, they have fueled public cynicism not just about the executive branch but also about the excessively partisan nature of Congress itself.

So what can be done? Congress needs to develop a continuous, systematic oversight process, which it now lacks, that impels congressional committees to look into the vast number of federal activities that never get into the newspaper headlines. Committee chairmen need a clear signal from the congressional leadership that oversight needs to be done in a much more thorough and bipartisan way.

But ultimately, much of the responsibility for putting Congress on the right track and for achieving the better policies that better oversight can bring lies with the American people. So the next time you see members of Congress getting headlines with some high-profile investigation, ask what they are also doing to review significant federal laws, agencies, and programs on a regular basis. It can't hurt to remind them that even overseers need oversight.

Improving Ethics Enforcement

Without a doubt, one of the least enjoyable tasks I had during my years in Congress was serving on the House Standards of Official Conduct Committee—the ethics committee. The hours are long, the rewards are few, and the task of sitting in judgment of colleagues is distasteful. Other members are uneasy about the fact that you are evaluating their behavior, and the work can take large chunks of time away from important legislative and constituent duties. It is certainly not an assignment that members seek.

In my own case, I was standing in the rain one evening in downtown Washington trying to hail a taxi after a long meeting. It was a heavy rain, and I was not having any luck. Then up drove a big limousine. The window rolled down, and there was Tip O'Neill offering me a ride back to the Hill. I told him how very grateful I was. He asked me to serve on the Standards Committee, and that was that. Ever since, I've made a point of driving myself to Washington events.

Yet despite all the negatives, I still feel it was one of the most important things I did—working to maintain the highest standards of congressional conduct.

Why is that important? It's not that we took any particular pleasure in finding fault or meting out punishment. Rather, it goes to the very heart of our system of representative democracy, which depends upon the confidence of the people in the basic integrity of their elected representatives. The public needs to have confidence that legislators are working for the common good, rather than for their own personal enrichment or for someone currying favor through gifts or special benefits. The purpose of tough ethics enforcement is less to punish a member than to protect the integrity of the Congress.

The duty of Congress to police its membership comes directly from the Constitution, as Article 1, Section 5 authorizes each house of Congress to "punish its Members for disorderly behavior and, with the concurrence of two-thirds, expel a Member." The first recorded instance of the House attempting to take disciplinary action was in 1798, when a vote to expel a member for spitting on another fell just short of the two-thirds needed for expulsion. Since then, misconduct cases have ranged from dueling, bribery, and treason in the Civil War era to pocketing official funds and inserting obscene material into the *Congressional Record*. When I was on the committee, several members of Congress had to leave office because of influence peddling.

The situation has improved significantly since I first came to Congress. A code of official conduct has been formalized as well as toughened from time to time. The ethics committee was established, and much more attention has been given to preventive ethics—trying to head off misconduct before it occurs. I was pleased to have been involved in many of these reforms. But although improvements have been made, more needs to be done. There is a rhythm to the work of the congressional ethics committees—sometimes they are tough, sometimes less so. Periods of reform are followed by backtracking, as in the recent change no longer allowing outside watchdog groups to file complaints about a member's conduct. Congress is still searching for the proper role of the committees and the appropriate level of ethics enforcement.

What I've found particularly distressing is that in recent years the standard has increasingly become whether the senator or representative violated the criminal law. Unless a member commits a felony and is convicted in the courts, the committee is often reluctant to act. That is not a satisfactory standard.

In disciplining members, the basic concern should be maintaining high standards of official conduct. This is not the same as trying to determine whether something is illegal. The basic test is not "Did the action violate the law?" but rather "Did the action reflect discredit on the Congress or call into question the member's ability to perform his official duties?" That is a higher and broader standard than the criminal law, and it is captured in the basic precept, well stated in Rule 1 of the House Code of Official Conduct, that the central responsibility of members is to conduct themselves "at all times in a manner which shall reflect creditably on the House of Representatives." The ethics committees have broad discretion to take action against a wide range of misconduct—not just illegal acts—that undermines the integrity of Congress.

Congress often loses sight of this basic test, instead getting caught up in legalistic debates over complex regulations. A few years ago, one of the Standards Committee's conclusions about a member was that he violated House ethics standards both by arranging questionable personal trips and by using a telephone to do it. Perhaps in the legal world the use of a telephone in interstate trafficking makes a difference, but to say that phone use indicates a violation of basic House ethics norms shows how far we have strayed from the essence of the Code of Conduct.

Maintaining high standards of conduct needs to be a continual focus of Congress and a higher institutional priority. For their part, legislators need always to keep in mind their fundamental responsibility never to act in ways that bring discredit on Congress. Our country's founders recognized that no matter how well-structured government is, it will not work unless its offices are held by people of virtue. Many times I have been reminded of the wisdom of Thomas Jefferson's statement that "the whole art of government consists in the art of being honest."

During my years in the House I gained great respect for the kind of men and women who serve in Congress. I found the vast majority of my colleagues to be honest and hardworking, trying to do their best for their constituents and for the nation. It was, indeed, a privilege to serve with them. That's why it is particularly important for Congress to make sure that any official misconduct by a member of Congress will not be tolerated, to prevent the integrity of the institution as a whole from being tarnished by the actions of a few.

When I traveled around southern Indiana meeting with constituents, I found that people wanted their political leaders to possess sound character, above virtually any other trait. They had it right. Maintaining high standards of congressional conduct helps to reinforce public accountability and helps to reestablish trust in an institution that touches on the lives of every American. If we have confidence in the judgment and integrity of our leaders, our representative democracy is enhanced.

Thinking about the Future

As a member of Congress, I got pretty good at responding when people criticized the institution. Congress ignores the views of citizens? Actually, I liked to say, sometimes it pays too much attention to the latest polls. Congress is irrelevant to ordinary people's lives? Which federally funded highway, I'd reply, had my critic used to get to this meeting?

But there was one reproach for which I had—and still have—no ready response. "You folks can't think beyond the next election," I was sometimes told, and all I could do was nod my head in agreement. The basic fact is that Congress—and for that matter, the federal government—just is not very good at identifying and dealing with future challenges. I recently reread a speech I gave in 1973 on the need for energy independence; I could give the same speech today, almost word for word.

There is a raft of difficult questions that our nation's legislators ought to be focusing considerable attention on, but are not. What will be the size and composition of the American population in ten, twenty, forty years? What are the biggest projected demographic shifts, and what impact will they have? What are the consequences of the growing number of unemployable youth in our increasingly technological society, as well as the growing number of the oldest members in our society and their increased need of services? What can we do to ensure we have adequate food, energy, and water supplies well into the future? What can be done to reduce the threat of both new and reemerging diseases? Will there be major consequences from the growing economic inequality within the nation, as well as between the United States and other nations? What fundamental challenges will we face to maintaining an economy that is both prosperous and free, and what might be new future threats to our national security? What changes will be needed to ease our government into the twenty-first century?

These are not pie-in-the-sky questions. They are issues that will affect the nature and quality of our lives sooner than we think, and it would be much better not to have to address them when we're in a crisis. Unlike many businesses, Congress does little strategic, long-term planning. Indeed, in recent years it has taken steps that reduce its capability, for example, eliminating both the Congressional Clearinghouse on the Future and the Office of Technology Assessment, which analyzed various proposals with a particular eye to their long-range implications.

A few years ago, a careful observer of Congress told me something quite wise. The very worst thing about congressional service, he said, is that members never have time to put their feet up on their desks, look out the window, and think about the long-term challenges coming at us down the road.

Why is this? Partly it has to do with the election cycle: Politicians face a constant press of campaigning and fund-raising, and campaigns for political office are pretty much endless these days. The same is true of the budget cycle: Our government works on a one-year cycle, which means that much of its time is dominated by putting together the budget, giving politicians little time to think about the future. And when Congress is not trying to find its way out of the latest budget crisis, it is turning its attention to some immediate problem, whether it is relief for a wildfire in the Southwest or an outbreak of disease in China. Not surprisingly, constituents and media commentators reinforce this habit: They want action on the problems that confront them at the moment. Members face relentless demands from constituents and communities.

I remember once being in the office of President Clinton's national security advisor, Tony Lake, and asking him about the large stack of files on his desk. "Those files all deserve immediate attention. They cannot wait," he replied. Then I noticed an even larger stack, probably twice as high, piled up behind him. "Those," he said, "are extremely urgent."

That anecdote pretty well sums up the problem that has become known in Washington as "the tyranny of the inbox." The day-to-day problems are so many, and so pressing, that the policymaker cannot free himself to do much thinking about future challenges.

Thomas Jefferson, in his first inaugural address, spoke eloquently of judging how our actions would affect the "thousandth generation." How do we promote more long-term thinking in Congress and a greater willingness to grapple with the tough issues that face us beyond the next election? For one thing, I believe it would be helpful to require the president to report every few years on the critical challenges facing the nation in future decades. Such a report could provide a useful focus for a wide-ranging discussion of long-range challenges, both within Congress and across the country. I also think that Congress should move to biennial budgeting. By enacting most budget legislation once every two years, instead of every year, it would reduce workloads and give federal agencies and Congress more time to look ahead to long-range needs.

But above all, I think members of Congress need encouragement to make long-range thinking a greater personal priority. Most members believe it doesn't matter much to their constituents. So the next time you happen to be at some event with your congressional representative, don't just criticize "Congress" for not thinking "beyond the next election." Ask your representative how much time he or she sets aside to look into the problems that will be confronting us in the next decade and beyond, problems that will matter not just to you but also to your children and their future.

The Money Chase

One revealing comment that the experts make in assessing political races is "Follow the money." If you know relatively little about a particular race or if it seems too close to call, look to see which candidate has raised the most money and that's your likely winner. That's not invariably true, but it usually is.

In contrast to the limited public interest in better congressional oversight or in more long-term thinking, people will often comment to me about the role of money in politics and the high cost of running for Congress. That concern is anything but new. Indeed, even before the Congress was set up, the founders were worried about the large amount of money it would take to run for a House seat.

As the costs of running for Congress have skyrocketed, particularly with the high price of television ads, members of Congress must spend an enormous amount of time fund-raising. Raising $4 million for an average Senate campaign, for example, means raising $15,000 *every week* over the senator's six-year term. The money chase distorts the political process, crowding out other activities like writing laws, thinking about public policy, or meeting with ordinary voters. It can also be an unpleasant task. Hubert Humphrey once called the chase for campaign money "a disgusting, degrading, demeaning experience."[3] The large amount of time and effort required for fund-raising was not the main factor in my decision to finally leave Congress, but it wasn't an insignificant consideration either.

The current system also has a major impact on challengers. The large amount of money needed to run a competitive campaign discourages many strong potential candidates who don't have personal wealth to pump into a campaign or who don't want to spend large chunks of their time fund-raising. Incumbents know that the way to scare off competition is to raise a lot of money, and it has become a chief campaign tactic.

In addition, many who contribute money are concerned about a "shakedown" atmosphere. They often feel that they cannot get their views across unless they contribute generously to politicians they may dislike. The common feature of the great debates in Congress over the past few years—including health care reform and changes to the tax code—is that they were all awash with money. Members used these debates skillfully to get money from people who were interested in certain legislative outcomes, and the donors used their contribution to gain access to members and to encourage them to see their issues in a sympathetic light. Such access does not guarantee his or her vote. However, even the mere appearance of a quid pro quo results in damage to the institution's reputation.

The rising flood of money that flows into campaigns also undermines general public trust in the political system. Many Americans feel it is money, not ideas and not principles, that reigns supreme in our political system. I often heard people say that the political process was run by the moneyed interests, so they saw little reason to vote. Cynicism is always the worst enemy of democracy, and it has certainly been bolstered by the way we finance campaigns.

Changing the campaign finance system is terribly difficult. The blunt fact is that most members of Congress and both political parties prefer the system under which they were elected over some untested scheme that might replace it. It is a system they know how to make work to their advantage and under which they have risen to the top. They are understandably reluctant to change it. Moreover, it is very difficult to devise a system that will reduce the disproportionate influence of money in politics and still not trample on constitutional rights to express political views. Historians of Congress have noted that the ingenuity of donors and the needs of candidates have hindered almost every attempt to curb high campaign spending,[4] and I think that's an accurate assessment. Campaign finance reform is very much like trying to reduce the size of a balloon by squeezing one side of it.

Our lack of effective campaign laws in this country represents a major failure in American public policy. It diverts members' attention, makes races less competitive by scaring off strong potential candidates, and raises doubts about the integrity of the legislative process. We have a campaign finance system today that is broken and gradually eroding the public's trust and confidence. It is a slow-motion crisis, but it is a crisis.

Various steps will be helpful, such as providing complete disclosure of all campaign contributions. But my basic view is that the only real solution will involve partial public financing of congressional elections, as we have done for the presidential elections and as many other nations and several states do for their legislative races. Providing an appropriate level of public funds for candidates limits overall spending, takes some of the immensely time-consuming burden of fund-raising away from candidates, makes elections more competitive, and reduces the power of well-funded interest groups. I understand that my view is not popular and that providing taxpayer funds for congressional races is a tough sell with the public. But I believe it will become more popular as people gradually come to understand the powerful influence of money on the process and the extent to which money undermines representative democracy and a government of, by, and for the people.

But as we try to reform the system, we must not let the perfect be the enemy of the good. It is not possible to enact a perfect, sweeping campaign finance reform bill today, and perhaps not anytime soon. Yet the worst abuses can be dealt with, one by one. Just as Congress and the president did with the recent curbs on "soft money" contributions to political parties, we simply must keep at it and address the abuses and plug the loopholes in the law as they become evident. A long journey proceeds one step at a time.

Improving Public Understanding of Congress

One of the ironies about Congress is that while the legislative system put in place by the framers has served our nation well for more than two hundred years, many of its essential components are not at all popular with the general public.

Americans like quick action rather than delay. They don't like dispute and a lot of arguing. And they don't like compromise, which they feel means selling out. Yet, as I've mentioned, these are precisely the features of our system of representative democracy that have allowed it to work so well in our large country: proceeding deliberately so all sides have a chance to be heard on often very complicated issues; providing for a free and open, even sometimes heated, debate on the merits of the issues; and then trying to reach a broadly acceptable consensus through a process of negotiation, give-and-take, and compromise. As political scientists have pointed out, much of what the public dislikes about Congress is endemic to what a legislature is.[5] Americans strongly support representative democracy in the abstract, but they dislike the untidiness of its legislative process just as strongly.

It would have been easy for the framers to create a quick, efficient, tidy system, giving all the power to a single ruler. But this nation was started by people who were fed up with living under a government commanded from the top. Instead they wanted a system that would let the voice of the people drive the government. So they divided up rather than concentrated powers and set up a Congress essentially charged with reconciling our nation's many points of view on the great public policy issues of the day. That's why Congress often takes its time about things. For the framers, fully airing differences, proceeding slowly and carefully, engaging in extensive negotiation, and reaching compromise are the essentials of how the system is supposed to work, not the grounds for cynicism and despair.

In a representative democracy, which depends so heavily upon the trust of the governed, it really does matter what people think about Congress. Yet one of the things I've come to realize over the years is that Congress does a lousy job of explaining to the public how it operates and why. There are no fancy brochures about how it works, no central information office responding to institutional criticisms, no positive ads or catchy slogans about its mission. Even the millions of tourists who visit the Capitol each year are educated more about the statues of dead Americans they pass in the hallways than about the essentials of how Congress works. And more often than not, legislators will run for Congress by running against Congress—saying, yes, it's a mess, and I'm working to try to clean it up—rather than trying to defend the institution. One thing every member of Congress quickly learns is that it is the simplest thing in the world to make yourself look good and the institution of the Congress look bad.

Better efforts are needed on all fronts—from legislators, from the media covering Congress, from civic educators—to improve public understanding of Congress, especially about the appropriate untidiness of the legislative process. The new Capitol Visitor Center being developed, for example, is an important step in the right direction. What may be elementary and obvious to those who follow Congress closely is not obvious to many Americans, who may perceive only dimly what Congress is all about. Congress can increase public support by implementing needed reforms, but it can also increase support by doing a better job of explaining what it does, how it works, and why it matters in people's lives.

Tackling the Tough Issues

Recently I gave a speech about Congress and how it operates, and afterwards someone from the audience came up to me, unhappy. "You are too generous," he said. "I'm disappointed in Congress every day." My critic had a good point. Anyone who follows Congress has been disappointed with its work—maybe not every day, but probably more than occasionally.

People would often complain about the power of special interests or the partisan bickering. But one of my chief disappointments with Congress is that it often does not deal head-on with the biggest, most difficult problems facing our country—problems such as the large number of Americans without health insurance, the long-term threats to the solvency of Social Security, and the failure to reduce dependence on foreign energy sources. Too often, Congress puts off doing anything substantive about these and other big issues, resorting instead to posturing and speechmaking, trying to make people believe that real action is occurring when, in fact, it is not. In the House and the Senate, a lot of time gets wasted with members from one party blaming the other for the failure to get anything done.

Sometimes when confronted with a difficult problem, Congress spends its energy dealing with it only on the margins. Take, for example, the recent congressional debate over setting up a Patients' Bill of Rights. There's no question that some patients suffer at the hands of health care providers whose zeal to cut costs leads to substandard care. But such abuse is just one of the problems in the American health care system—and not the biggest one at that. Congress needs to take a more comprehensive approach to reforming the health care system, dealing first with its most glaring flaw—that millions of people cannot afford any medical treatment at all because they have no health care insurance.

This practice has even gotten its own title from political observers—"surrogate issue," the congressional habit of working on one small piece of a problem while leaving the bigger issue unresolved. It is a practice that often frustrates members of Congress themselves. A commonly heard question among members on the floor is why some minor bill is coming up when there are so many huge problems facing the nation.

I certainly don't want to say that Congress never tackles tough issues. During my time in Congress, the 1983 Social Security rescue package and the 1986 tax reform act were examples of Congress grappling with complicated, politically sensitive issues and ultimately passing very important legislation. But overall, the record of Congress over the past several decades in addressing the biggest challenges facing our country has been mixed at best.

Serious obstacles stand in the way of Congress as it seeks to deal with the nation's thorniest problems. Solutions are not easy to devise, because there often is not one clearly correct way to address the problem. Liberals may prefer more active government involvement in addressing a problem, whereas conservatives typically prefer a remedy that encourages the private sector to devise a solution. Either course might work, but serious people of differing views naturally will debate at length over the proper path for Congress to pursue.

Moreover, our system of government was not set up for quick action, especially on tough issues where there is no clear societal consensus about the correct response. The framers of our Constitution wanted to make sure that all sides would have an opportunity to be heard and that there would be time for negotiation and compromise, instead of letting a majority push controversial measures through quickly. Congress can act quickly when there is a national consensus. But when there are deep divisions in the country, this is reflected in the Congress.

None of this excuses Congress. Taking on the tough issues is its responsibility. If Congress does not deal with them, how are they going to be solved?

There is no simple remedy to getting more congressional focus on the really big issues. Much of it is up to the leadership. For their part, members need to be less partisan and more pragmatic, focusing more on finding solutions and less on hewing to an ideologically or politically pure line. But voters also have a role to play in helping Congress solve the big problems. They must give members of Congress a clear signal over a sustained period of time that action on these key national challenges is both needed and expected.

Congress and the Common Good

Not long ago, a journalist asked what worries me most about Congress. I paused for a moment to consider the question, and as I did so, an old political encounter sprang to mind.

It was Election Day, and I was back in the southern Indiana district I represented in Congress, making the rounds of voting precincts and chatting with voters. Outside, I ran into an older woman I'd never met, and I asked whether she had voted. She said she had, and then added, "You know, I vote for my candidate, and then I go home and pray for the winner." I asked her what she meant. "Well, I want him or her to work not just for a few," she said, "but for everyone."

I never did meet that woman again, but her comments have stuck with me all these years. In that brief comment, I thought, she expressed the healthiest attitude toward politics I had ever heard, and she said it better than any politician or pundit. I think it's what most of us want: that our elected representatives work not just for a few, but for everyone.

But Congress, I told my interviewer, doesn't do it enough. It does not focus sufficiently on the common good. There are lots of reasons for this, some of them quite understandable. As a member of Congress, for instance, you might have fifteen meetings a day, and every single one will be with someone who wants his or her slice of the federal budget. There are farmers and small-businesspeople and defense contractors and researchers and road-builders and people who suffer from disease. There's a myriad of interest groups, corporations, unions, professional groups, constituents, and colleagues, all of whom want just that one little bit of the federal dollar and who can make an eloquent case that it may benefit them personally, but really, it will benefit the nation as a whole.

There's nothing sinister or malicious about any of this; in a sense, it's how the process of government works: Out of the clamor of different voices and divergent needs, we forge policy and a sense of direction. But I remember often sitting in those meetings and wondering, "Who speaks for the common good? Who stands apart from this agitated group of special-interest people and thinks about the good of the country?" This is not, by the way, a new question. Thomas Jefferson, in his first inaugural address, urged Americans "to unite in common efforts for the common good." And those who make policy, John Adams once wrote, should maintain a "disinterested attachment to the public good, exclusive and independent of all private and selfish interest." The founders spent a lot of time pondering ways to encourage this, and the system they came up with—separating the government into three coequal branches—was designed with that goal in mind. Thinking about the good of the country, in other words, is the job of the Congress no less than that of the president and the Supreme Court. All too often, though, it falls short.

There is no single force to blame for this. The high-stakes gamesmanship of politics today, the influence of campaign money, the sophisticated strategies of lobbyists, the growing complexity and scope of legislation, the sheer demands on the time and energy of members of Congress, the extraordinary diversity of the American people—all make it difficult for an individual member of Congress to step back and sort through what he or she believes is right for the country. And why do so when you don't need to? Please enough self-interested groups, and you've hammered together a majority. That's considered to be realistic congressional politics these days, and there are those who argue that it's the way things ought to be. Everybody working for his or her own self-interest, they argue, is what makes this country work.

But I don't think that's what Adams or Jefferson had in mind. Seeking to please as many groups as possible may be how you gain or hold on to power, but it is not how you govern wisely. I can't help but think that the remedy for much that ails our political system is for each of us—ordinary citizen and member of Congress alike—to restore in our lives a sense of the public good, to ask ourselves not what's good for any one of us but what's good for the country.

I once met a historian who had extensively studied Franklin Delano Roosevelt. "I'm a Democrat," I said, "but the truth is, I don't know a lot about Roosevelt. What should we remember about him?" The response came without hesitation: "Roosevelt judged every piece of legislation by the question, How does it affect ordinary people?" That's the right test, and it's the one every member of Congress should apply.

Conclusion

I've recommended a lot of changes and suggested several ways in which the operations of Congress could be improved. But I certainly don't want to give the impression that I believe Congress is falling apart or in shambles. Indeed, I firmly believe that the basic way the framers set it up has served us well. The core structure that has been in place for two hundred years works even today. Our system of representative democracy has displayed a remarkable resilience and underlying strength. Congress needs reforms, but we do not need a radical overhaul of our institutions.

There is one more way in which I think Congress could work better—by improving the dialogue between the represented and the representative. To me, that lies at the heart of what representative democracy is all about. And exploring it is the topic of chapter 6.

6

Civic Participation

OUR SYSTEM OF GOVERNMENT places special responsibilities on us. Justice Felix Frankfurter called
citizenship "the highest office" in the land. A representative democracy is based upon the idea of citizen participation—the notion
that ordinary people have both the right and the responsibility to
be involved in their governance. And Congress, in particular, was
set up to be the branch most connected to the American people's
interests, hopes, and aspirations.

Yet Americans are of two minds when it comes to citizen participation. By wide margins they strongly support our system of
government and recognize the importance of civic involvement. But
by equally wide margins they are spectators rather than participants,
increasingly not writing their elected representatives, not voting,
not turning out for public meetings.

As Walter Lippmann pointed out: "We are concerned in public
affairs, but immersed in our private ones."[1] People lead busy lives
and are often cynical about government and skeptical about the
responsiveness of political leaders. So if they feel that their voices

just don't matter, why should they bother? This chapter will explore various ways in which Americans can become engaged in the work of Congress and sort out the core elements of good citizenship.

A Failure to Communicate

A bit over two decades ago, in a plain, cinder-block community hall in Switzerland County, Indiana, I got a lesson in democracy that bears remembering. Switzerland County is a deeply rural, tobacco-growing area in the far southern corner of the state, and in the late 1970s it was about as rustic a setting as you could find in Indiana. Certainly it was not a place I expected to come for enlightenment on international politics.

While I was meeting with a group of constituents, though, the subject of the Panama Canal treaties came up, well before the national media had focused on the issue. A man I'd never met suddenly stood up and proceeded to lay out the cleanest, clearest, most evenly reasoned argument for ratification that I ever did hear on the matter. I was flabbergasted, but took it as a humbling reminder that as a member of Congress, you can always find constituents who know more about a given subject than you.

More recently, however, I've begun to see even more cogent lessons in that long-ago encounter. It was, first, a bracing illustration of how much responsibility ordinary citizens bear for making Congress work properly.

This may seem an odd notion to suggest at a time when people feel increasingly estranged from their government in Washington, and criticizing Congress is now second nature to many people, as easy as griping about the IRS. For myself, I'm impressed with the way Congress tackles difficult national problems, acts as a national forum, mirrors a wide range of views, and over time usually develops a consensus that reflects the collective judgment of a diverse people. Yet the truth is that this can happen only if there is a conversation, a process of mutual education. Legislators have to be able to educate their constituents—illuminate issues, explain their own thinking, make clear that most issues are not black or white. And citizens have to be able to educate their representatives: The policies that Congress enacts will work only to the extent that they're grounded in the realities faced by ordinary Americans. All of this depends on open and trusting interaction between members of Congress and the people who elected them. This two-way conversation, with each educating the other, lies at the heart of what representative democracy is all about.

But the second lesson is that this interaction is increasingly hard to find these days. My constituent's statement was the kind of moment nicely captured in a Norman Rockwell painting but increasingly rare in real life. The overall figures on citizen participation are discouraging. Only about one in every seven adult Americans writes letters to members of Congress and one in eight attends political meetings. Only one in every four American adults reports paying attention to public affairs most of the time, and less than one in four will take an active part in a political organization. Only one in three can name their congressman, and even fewer can identify their positions on major issues. And for the past few congressional elections, only 45–50 percent of registered voters have turned out in presidential election years and 35–40 percent in nonpresidential election years. In some districts it's been below 20 percent. The dialogue between represented and representative that supports our system of government doesn't happen to nearly the extent it should.

Moreover, political scientists tell us there is a strong socioeconomic tilt in political participation. Citizens who are financially better off, more highly educated, with higher-status jobs participate much more in politics than other Americans. Arguably the very citizens who most need government assistance are the least likely to exercise political influence. This difference in political resources not only influences the kind of issues that dominate the political agenda but also undermines the widespread civic participation that is a cornerstone of representative democracy.

Some of the problem, no doubt, lies with Congress itself. Members find it increasingly difficult to reach out to the huge number of constituents they now represent for a meaningful and open dialogue. They also deal with so many complex issues now that they have trouble finding the time to consult regularly with their districts. A century ago, a member of Congress handled three or four weighty national issues over the course of a career; today, he or she may have to do the same thing before lunch. And when legislators do meet with their constituents, the temptation is to soften their comments rather than have a frank discussion about what is best for the country. Members are very good at that.

But some of the responsibility for this breakdown in communications also lies with ordinary citizens. Americans live busy lives and are often cynical about the responsiveness of government. As a result, many are giving up on the conversation. In my last few terms in office, the turnouts at public meetings, issue forums, and district office visits were all down, as were "real" letters unprompted by special interest groups. And more often than not, as I stood in front of a roomful of voters, I could feel a curtain of doubt hanging between me and them. They believed that I took the positions I did because of this or that campaign contribution, not because I had spent time studying and weighing the merits of issues. They gave themselves over to cynicism, and cynicism is the great enemy of democracy. It is very difficult for public officials to govern when their character, values, and motives are always suspect. It makes dialogue, conversation, and mutual education impossible.

At the Gettysburg battlefield some 140 years ago, Abraham Lincoln talked about a government "of the people, by the people, and for the people" and reflected on how the founders created "a new nation, conceived in liberty, and dedicated to the proposition that all men are created equal." As the Civil War raged, he asked "whether that nation, or any nation so conceived and so dedicated, can long endure." That question may put it in rather apocalyptic terms, but it nonetheless is on the mark. Nowhere is it written in the stars that the answer to Lincoln's question is forevermore a "yes." If citizen participation continues its downward slide, how long can we go on claiming that we truly have a representative democracy?

Congress is the most important link between the American people and their national government, the institution whose job it is to address the many views and needs of the people. But it can't operate—at least, not legitimately—without Americans' involvement. My constituent in Switzerland County, I think, understood this. He understood that the relationship between a citizen and a legislator requires a little time, thought, and effort. He understood that I could represent him only if we *had* a relationship—that in the cacophony of modern politics, a bit of clear thinking and calm discussion would carry his voice all the way back to Washington with me.

Being More Involved in the Work of Congress

People are often told in general terms to get more involved, but how exactly might they be more actively engaged in the work of Congress?

First and foremost is voting in congressional elections. Those votes not only determine who represents us in the House and Senate but also who controls Congress and who sets the legislative agenda. Americans know they should vote. A recent survey found that 82 percent of Americans recognized it as either an essential or very important obligation. And yet in recent years, most Americans have taken a pass on voting. During the years I was in Congress, turnout for congressional elections in nonpresidential election years dropped fairly steadily from just under 50 percent to closer to 35 percent.

Many people don't vote because they feel government isn't very responsive anymore or they think their vote doesn't count. Sometimes they feel the issues aren't important. Often people say they're discouraged from voting because politics is too partisan and because politicians have become captive to ideological extremists and special interest groups. What people must understand is that by not voting, they are helping create an environment in Washington that is contaminated by intense partisanship, one in which the power of ideological factions and special interests is amplified. These factions and interests make sure their faithful show up at the polls, so, naturally, candidates for elective office cater to them. Higher voter turnout is one of the best remedies for Washington's partisanship.

Several steps could be taken to spur voter turnout. To a significant extent, the problem of low voter turnout is one of low voter registration. Some states require people to register to vote many weeks in advance of an election, a practice long out of date in this era of instant data transmission via computers and the Internet. Polling hours are often inconvenient for working people with long commutes. In my home state of Indiana, for example, the polls close at 6:00 P.M., far too early for people who work a full day and then face a tough drive home. I also heard from older constituents who said they wouldn't vote because they found polling places intimidating—the signs, the workers, the candidates, the complicated machines.

We should also enact reforms that would help make our elections more competitive, especially contests for seats in the U.S. House of Representatives. In most elections, only a few dozen of the 435 seats in the House are seriously in play, so it's not surprising people think their vote doesn't count. We also need to break down the feeling of alienation that too many Americans feel toward the federal government. They see government as merely a taxing authority that does things to the people, rather than a helper that is of, by, and for the people.

Yet when you hear someone say, "My vote doesn't matter," don't nod in agreement. In the 2000 election, if just 2,750 votes had been different in various congressional races across the country, the House of Representatives would have gone to the other party. And in several House and Senate elections in recent years, we've seen the winner decided by less than $\frac{1}{10}$ of 1 percent of the votes cast. Every vote is important, not just because it can make a difference in a particular race but because it reaffirms the voter's basic confidence in our system of representative democracy.

But more than voting is needed. The Framers felt that citizens should vote and then largely leave it up to their elected representatives to carry out the activities of government. Yet over the years the notion of civic responsibility has been expanded. And for the past hundred years it has been recognized that a properly functioning representative democracy requires its citizens to do more than just show up at the polls for a few minutes every two years.

So here are several other ways in which you could be more engaged in the work of Congress:

• Learn about Congress. There are many good sources about Congress and how it works, from the traditional ones—newspapers, books, television—to some newer ones, such as e-mail updates, multimedia CD-ROMs, and interactive websites. Visit the websites of your representative and two senators to find out what they are doing and what positions they are taking. If you find their websites aren't very informative, which is possible, press them to do a better job. Learning more about Congress forms the basis for effective involvement. Voting is good, but informed voting is better.

• Meet with your member of Congress. When he or she holds a public meeting in town, show up and ask a question or make a point. And every member of Congress encourages constituents to meet with them in either their local or Washington office. Personal encounters with legislators are an especially effective way of communicating what is important to you.

• Write to your member of Congress. Constituent letters, e-mails, postcards, and petitions all can alert members to important needs and local priorities. Mail, rather than personal contact, is now the main link between legislators and their constituents.

• Participate "virtually" via the Internet. In recent years legislators have, for example, been holding electronic town meetings and providing easy e-mail links for constituents. Some have posted surveys soliciting the views of their constituents on specific issues that might be coming up for a vote. If yours does, take the time to fill it out. Cyberpolitics is a promising avenue for communication, especially for younger Americans, who in general tend to avoid traditional means of participation.

• Be involved with your political party. Revitalizing the parties is important because of their role in building consensus, empowering people from varied backgrounds, and balancing off narrow interest groups.

• Help with a candidate's campaign activities. Although Americans vote less than people in other democracies, they do participate more in various campaign-related activities, and giving money to candidates has increased significantly in recent years.

• Get involved with local issues, particularly projects of interest to your congressman. A good way to connect with members of Congress is to work with them on important local matters, from improving a road to strengthening civics education in the schools. Most members also have special projects, such as issues advisory groups, that need constituent involvement.

• Use the media to push your interests. This is an increasingly important strategy, given the influence the media have on our political system, and could include interesting a local reporter in your cause or writing a letter to the editor of your local paper. You'll be surprised at how many people pay attention, including your member of Congress.

• Join interest groups of like-minded people. Adding your voice to other voices will make it easier for your views to be heard in Washington. Joining interest groups—such as the AARP or NRA—is one of the few forms of civic participation that has increased in recent years, and it has increased sharply. Four-fifths of all Americans belong to at least one interest group.

• Participate in political demonstrations. Political activism has long played an important part in American politics.

The bottom line is that our system provides a host of opportunities for individuals to connect with their elected representatives and to participate in their governance. Having seen the benefits firsthand, I'm firmly on the side of those who favor broader participation. As Theodore Roosevelt said, "The credit goes to the man who is actually in the arena."[2]

The Cornerstones of Active Citizenship

All of us need to better understand the demands of democracy. But at the same time, we shouldn't overstate them. I've given a lot of suggestions, and I don't want to make people think that they aren't good citizens if they aren't poring over the *Congressional Record,* spending their evenings watching the House and Senate on C-SPAN, attending political meetings nonstop, or out organizing marches.

Not all of us have the time or the temperament to become extensively involved in public life; in fact, our system was set up to work without totally involved constituents—that's what our representatives are for. We do, after all, have a representative democracy rather than a direct democracy. Yet it is still the case that our system can't work unless ordinary people take enough of an interest in public life to give it direction and meaning. So which of all the items I've listed in the previous section are the really core elements of good citizenship, the steps I would single out as the most important for today's busy and often somewhat disengaged Americans?

The first is voting. Voting is one of the easiest things a citizen of this country can do to participate in American civic life. It is, in fact, the first of what I consider the four cornerstones of active citizenship. When you vote, of course, you are registering an opinion on whom you want representing you in Congress, in the White House, and at the state and local level. But you are doing other things as well. You are signaling something about your philosophy of government or, in elections that focus on a single issue, your opinion on that issue. More fundamentally, you are confirming your belief that it's *worth* voting—that you value a system that offers its citizens the chance to weigh in on the candidates and the issues of the day.

Elections are the great ritual of democracy, its single most important event. In this country they are hard fought, expensive, and increasingly complex. They involve many actors: candidates, consultants, political parties, interest groups, pollsters, volunteers.

And they have many features: media coverage, candidate debates, issue papers, campaign messages and themes, conventions, political organization. With all of the hoopla attending elections, it is easy to overlook their impact on the course of the country. Candidates make promises, and the winners try to carry theirs out. During the campaign candidates get a good idea of what voters want and don't want. These judgments eventually influence policy and mold legislation that affects all the people. Congress, for example, spends a lot more time on issues of interest to older Americans than on those important to young people, because seniors vote and are active participants.

But our democracy depends on us for more than simply casting our votes. So, secondly, our representatives also need to hear directly from us, either through letters or in person. On any given issue that comes up on Capitol Hill, you can bet they'll be hearing from lobbyists, special interest groups, their colleagues, and party leaders. That's certainly appropriate; it's part of how a good politician forms judgments. But in order for our representatives to do their jobs well, they also need to understand their constituents—to be familiar with our daily concerns, to appreciate our opinions, to recognize the subtleties of how we feel on the issues they confront.

This suggests, though, that we also have an obligation to understand those issues. This is why the third cornerstone of being an active citizen is to be informed about the problems we face, both as a nation and within our own communities. I'm not suggesting that this become your second job, but it helps to keep up on a regular basis with sources of information you trust. Just as parents at a community pool both chat and keep an eye on the scene, ready to dive in should something go wrong, so you should keep an informed eye on what's happening in Washington and be ready to respond if something suddenly troubles you.[3]

Just doing these three things—voting, keeping in touch with your representatives, and becoming informed about public issues—will take you a long way toward filling the role of a good citizen. But there's one more basic step we can take to give meaning to our democratic ideals: become involved in improving our own communities. It could be volunteering at a soup kitchen, helping build a house with Habitat for Humanity, manning the polls on Election Day, or making a railroad crossing safer—the *what* of it matters less than doing it.

Involvement is the greatest antidote to cynicism I know. Citizens who become engaged in community life no longer feel distant from the centers of power and decision making; they come to understand their own communities and to appreciate how they themselves can influence change. Perhaps most important, they gain an appreciation for the hard work of democracy—for how to build a consensus behind a particular course of action in a complex society. In that sense, they lessen the distance between themselves and their elected representatives and gain an understanding of, and appreciation for, civic life that can only make our society—and the ongoing experiment of American democracy—stronger.

Making Your Views Known to Congress

I once received a letter from a constituent that opened: "If you were only honest . . ." You can readily understand my reaction. This was—it's safe to say—not the most effective letter I ever received.

I think of that letter when I'm asked to explain to groups how they could most effectively talk to their elected representatives. Basically it's not all that difficult and varies little, if at all, from the way you communicate with your friends and neighbors. I recognize that many people say that the little guy just can't get heard in Washington anymore, that it takes well-paid lobbyists and expensive Washington receptions to catch the ear of a member of Congress. But lobbying can take very simple, and often much more effective, forms, such as meeting with your representative over a cup of coffee in the local café. You need not spend large amounts of money to make your case effectively with your member of Congress. On numerous occasions, conversations or letters from constituents have affected my approach to issues and brought new matters to my attention. Most Americans simply do not recognize the power they have to make a difference.

The methods of contacting members of Congress have changed considerably over the years. Throughout the early history of Congress, it was almost exclusively personal conversations between constituent and legislator back home. Even by 1900, for example, most members of Congress still didn't need any staff to help them with constituent letters. During the mid-1900s, constituent mail became the dominant means of communication, and in recent years the number of contacts has risen sharply, driven primarily by the use of computerized letter campaigns or preprinted postcards by interest groups. The number of letters and postcards received by the House now averages 115,000 *every day;* in the Senate, the figure is closer to 125,000.

Although the sacks of mail going in and out might suggest a vibrant dialogue between represented and representative, the fact is that most of it consists of form letters responding to form letters and computers talking to computers. In many congressional offices, identical form letters or postcards merely get counted or weighed. And it is still the case that the vast majority of Americans will go through their entire lives without once using any means—personal contact, letter, even preprinted postcard—to pass on a thought or opinion to their members of Congress, the people who are supposed to be representing their interests in Washington on a host of important matters.

Direct contact and personal letters remain two of the best ways for you to communicate with a member of Congress. Whatever your reason for making the contact—because you are having problems with a federal agency, your community needs a new road or bridge, or you feel strongly about a particular policy issue—you'll make more headway if you follow a few basic rules: Get your facts straight. Make your case concisely. Try to stick to a single issue, which can help focus the legislator's attention on your main concern. Give enough information so the legislator can understand both the issue and your views on it (often I'd be told to support a particular bill number, without any explanation of what the bill actually was). Be civil. Be timely. Write or call when the measure is still under active consideration. Try to learn what the member cares about and frame your contact in those terms. State clearly what you want your elected official to do. Be persistent. And if you are trying to persuade your congressman to approve or reject a piece of legislation, tell a personal story about how you think that bill would make your life better (or worse). Much more memorable and effective than mass mailings are messages that reflect direct personal experience.

There are also a few things you should probably try to avoid. Threatening a legislator is generally not effective, such as saying you and all of your family will vote against him or her because of their stance on a particular issue. Members don't mind tough language. They are accustomed to it, and it gives them a sense of the intensity of the voter. But letters that impugn the integrity or motives of a member or use pressure or the threat of retaliation are given less weight than those that deal with the substance of the question. A cool-headed and thoughtful approach is usually the best one.

Another generally unsuccessful tactic is going overboard in the number of contacts, thinking more is always better, such as packing a public meeting with one person after another to make the same point or clogging the office phone lines with hundreds of callers. It is helpful for members to know that a group of their constituents feels strongly about an issue, but at some point such tactics become disruptive and counterproductive. Unique and personal expressions of opinion are more effective than obviously orchestrated communication.

You should also be careful about linking your discussion of an issue with a mention of your campaign contributions. There are tough rules for members of Congress against doing anything in exchange for campaign contributions, and many legislators will feel insulted by even the hint that a quid pro quo is possible.

Being deceptive or misleading is also a mistake. Legislators understand that people will sometimes get the facts wrong, but letters filled with distortions and misleading statements will quickly be discounted.

So a clear, courteous, and succinct message has the most impact. Then once you have gotten in touch with a legislator about an issue of importance to you, what sort of response might you get? Several years ago I asked the Speaker of the House how he answered his mail. He said that answering the mail is very important and that he always sent out the same letter to everybody: "Thank you very much for your comments. I will take them into consideration." You will almost certainly get a more detailed response than that today. Yet what you hear back may still seem somewhat noncommittal to you.

One reason is that members are very much aware that legislation can change considerably as it moves through Congress. So they will rarely commit themselves early on and tell you that, yes, they will vote for a specific bill. I remember Congressman Mo Udall recounting how a bill he had introduced and was particularly keen about had been amended so many times as it moved through Congress that even he ended up voting against "the Udall bill." Members may also sometimes be withholding judgment until they get a better sense of the views of more of their constituents. I had particular difficulty, for example, in reaching and hearing from young parents, who were often too busy with jobs and children to participate in community activities. Sometimes the issues are just very difficult, and legislators want more time for deliberation and consultation. So you shouldn't try to force a member to take a stand on an issue prematurely.

You should also keep in mind that communication is a two-way process. As you talk to your representatives in Congress, don't forget to listen to what they say or write. You might learn how to better influence them, but you will also probably learn that the issues are not as clear-cut as you believed. You will find that members weigh many competing opinions and interests when they vote—including the national interest—and are not simply swayed by big campaign contributions, special-interest lobbying, or one group of vocal constituents.

One other thing: You will probably enjoy the process of participation and gain a measure of satisfaction that you are doing your part as a good citizen. You may feel that you are having an impact and find that you are not quite as cynical about the process as you once were. Almost certainly you will recognize that government is not some alien force; it is you, me, all of us. And we all have the right, the responsibility, and the capacity to influence its course.

Individuals Who Have Made a Difference

Many years ago, shortly after I'd been reelected to Congress, a neighbor of mine crossed the street and knocked on my door. I didn't know the man very well, just enough to stop and chat briefly as our paths crossed from time to time, but now he had something significant to say.

He was, he told me, a diabetic. And he was flummoxed by the packaged food he tried to buy at the grocery store. He had no idea what was actually in it. This was the mid-1960s; food manufacturers didn't have to label what they put in their products. "I go to the supermarket, and I simply don't know what's in those packages," he said. "I want you to do something about labeling." I told him I'd look into it.

Many people would have stopped right there, figuring they'd gotten the attention of someone in a position to do something; fortunately, my neighbor knew that wasn't enough. He talked the issue up in the community, spent his lunches and evenings giving talks to service clubs, visited and wrote letters to all sorts of politicians—members of the county commission, state legislators in Indianapolis, other members of Congress. Over time, thanks to his efforts and those of a lot of other people who were of a similar mind, the issue blossomed and consumers now have meaningful labels on the food they buy.

Individuals can and do make a difference in a host of ways. History is full of examples of ordinary people who have had a major impact on our political system, even from its very beginning. James Madison, for example, was an ordinary young man who was neither rich nor powerful. He was not well known or a great orator. But while still in his twenties he was sent to represent Virginia in the Continental Congress of 1780, and largely through the clarity of his thinking he became the preeminent figure at the convention and the main architect of our system of government.

Even in recent decades, when public cynicism has run high, there are many prominent examples of individuals who have made a difference. Most of us are familiar with the stories of Rosa Parks, or Erin Brockovich, or Howard Jarvis, the former businessman who started the Proposition 13 tax revolt in California. But it doesn't take much searching to come up with others.[4]

• In 1982, Gregory Watson was a student at the University of Texas who was upset about the low grade he got on a paper claiming that a constitutional amendment proposed in 1789 to prohibit members of Congress from raising their pay immediately without an intervening election had merit and could still be ratified. He single-handedly began to lobby various states to complete ratification of the amendment, which had been pending for almost two hundred years. Support for the amendment broadened, and in 1992 it became the Twenty-seventh Amendment to the Constitution.

• Jody Williams was a former schoolteacher and relief worker who in 1991 helped start from scratch an effort to prohibit the use of landmines, which can remain hidden long after a war is over, only to be triggered years later by someone working or playing in the field. Her determined work led to an international treaty signed by 122 countries that bans the use of landmines, and in 1997 she received the Nobel Peace Prize for her efforts.

• In 1967, Sally Reed wanted to administer the estate of her young son, who had just died. Yet her former husband was named administrator because under Idaho law "males must be preferred to females" when parents have equal claims. Even though the value of the estate was minimal, she challenged the decision as unfair, and in 1971 the U.S. Supreme Court unanimously reached its landmark decision against gender discrimination.

• In 1988, Merrell Williams was a part-time paralegal at a law firm that represented a large tobacco company. Although the tobacco industry had for years denied any link between smoking and disease, Williams secretly copied 4,000 documents that showed they knew otherwise. The documents became key pieces of evidence that resulted in the $400 billion settlement reached in 1999 between the tobacco companies and the states.

• Candy Lightner was a California mother who responded to the death of her thirteen-year-old daughter at the hands of a drunk driver by forming Mothers Against Drunk Driving (MADD) in 1980. Soon there were hundreds of local MADD chapters all working for tougher sentences for drunk drivers and for a higher minimum drinking age. For Lightner's leadership, President Reagan invited her to the White House in 1984 for the signing of a new law that soon resulted in every state having a drinking age of twenty-one.

All of these people were ordinary citizens who made extraordinary contributions. They felt very strongly about a particular matter and resolved that something had to be done. They were persistent, presented their case well, enlisted the support of others, and brought about important change, even surprising themselves with how much could be accomplished.

Such efforts can be done on a smaller scale, too, in local towns and communities across the country. Healthy communities depend upon people who have this sense of obligation to give back something to the free society of which they are a part. This is one of the core elements of good citizenship, and participants gain considerable satisfaction from their involvement. Over the years I've found that a person who is deeply involved in strengthening a school board, making an intersection safer, cleaning up a local stream, or helping children who go to bed hungry is rarely cynical and rarely disengaged from our system of government.

Certainly this takes some time and some commitment, which is often not easy for many of us. Some of the obstacles are beyond our immediate control—an economy that requires both parents in many families to work, a sprawling pattern of growth that shifts time from the community to the commute. But at its heart, I think, the question is one of attitude: If you believe you can make a difference, you'll find a way to do it. There are problems in every community that need to be addressed and many tangible, immediate ways that you can have an impact. If you haven't been involved in civic life, then the only way to prove to yourself that it matters is to go ahead and join in. Representative democracy requires each of us to do our part in whatever way we can.

As we'll see in the next section, there is another way people can make a difference, in a broader and even more basic way.

Can the People Govern?

Ask someone to define our democracy, and I'll bet he or she quotes Abraham Lincoln back to you. "Government of the people, by the people, and for the people" is how the sixteenth president put it in the Gettysburg Address.

But do these words really mean much these days? With Americans increasingly disengaged from the work of government and questioning why they should bother to communicate with their elected representatives, President Lincoln's words today sometimes seem to ring a little hollow. But as someone who's spent a lifetime in politics, I believe they're not. It's just that we need to think about them a bit differently than you might imagine.

There are two ways of looking at Lincoln's definition of democracy. One way—the usual way—is to think of "the people" as individuals, who try through one means or another to impact the political process. The other way is to imagine citizens not as a collection of individuals but as a community.

As individuals, it's true, our influence on the government can be somewhat limited. Certainly some individuals do have an impact in many constructive ways—pressing their member of Congress to address a local problem, mobilizing effective lobbying efforts, or arguing thoughtfully for a particular policy alternative, as my Panama Canal interlocutor did. Many Americans do make important contributions that way, although it's still a relatively modest number.

At the same time, I'm increasingly impressed by the way in which the people *as a community* have an impact and have it regularly. As a community of people who reside in this great nation, we share certain core values and have certain views about what should be on the national agenda. These values and basic ideas shape over time a collective opinion that politicians ignore at their peril.

Let's take our values. By overwhelming margins, Americans support our Constitution and the system of government it creates giving a central voice to the people. They also believe everyone should have an equal opportunity to succeed, retain a deep respect for capitalism, and have a strong sense of fairness and decency. Americans feel they should be able to live their lives without constant fear of crime, have access to basic medical care when they need it, and be able to eat safe food, drink safe water, and breathe safe air. The people convey these and other values to their elected representatives, and they want government policies to reflect those values.

The guidance, it's true, can be broad, and public policy issues can be complex and numerous. Legislators searching for the people's wisdom on current issues aren't going to find much guidance on questions like whether patients ought to be suing their HMOs in the federal courts or in the state courts. But the basic message from the people does come across clearly. For example, members are well aware that they will hear from their constituents if a proposed tax cut violates the public's sense of fairness, favoring one particular group rather than treating all fairly.

In a very real sense, contact from constituents helps set the agenda of Congress. A few years back, for instance, whenever I went home to meet with voters, people stood up in meeting after meeting and talked about public education. I'd been in Congress for twenty-five years, and in all that time I doubt the subject came up on more than a handful of occasions; it was a state issue, or a local matter, and no one figured their representative in Washington had much to do with it. But suddenly, concern about public schools had reached such a pitch that the issue crystallized in people's minds as a matter for the federal government. Now it's a front-burner item on Capitol Hill. Time and again, "the people" are able to direct the attention of elected representatives to the problems and concerns they want government to address. When public opinion coalesces on an issue, rarely do politicians ignore it. This sort of input is enormously important to members, and it is the sort of input that all of us can provide, if not regularly, at least periodically.

Congress is often portrayed as unresponsive, but I would suggest that Congress follows quite closely the clear and dominant moods of the country. In recent years, for example, Congress has shown sensitivity to the national moods against high taxes, against cuts in seniors programs, and against a weakened national defense, by supporting tax reductions, protecting Social Security benefits, and providing additional defense spending. Whatever Congress's shortcomings, I believe it has represented the people in these broad directions of public policy.

The responsiveness of Congress, of course, can be overstated. Given the number of interests in the country, Congress cannot and does not answer all of them. But overall, members of Congress strive to represent their constituents' interests as they understand those interests and as they have been communicated to them by the people.

So Lincoln's definition of democracy is right, especially when "the people" are viewed as a community that conveys important broad messages about values, fundamental ideas, and the policy agenda to their elected officials. In the end it really is a government of, by, and for the people.

Strengthening Representative Democracy

When I traveled through my southern Indiana district, I could always count on one thing: Whatever the town, every morning I would find locals gathered at some coffee shop or café to discuss and resolve the great issues of state and nation. In a good-natured way, they would kid me that they could solve the country's problems better than Congress.

I always came away from these sessions with a larger lesson— that the health of our democracy is sustained by these informal discussions among citizens. These sessions are replicated countless times across the country. At barbershops, in grocery store aisles, on the sidelines of kids' ball games, during PTA meetings, and at community and religious functions, public issues come up in an almost offhand way, interwoven with social chatter. The participants may not always be aware that they are part of Jefferson's "dialogue of democracy," the perpetual exchange that keeps the United States strong and prosperous and its people content and free, but they are.

Fundamentally, democracy is a process of mutual education—citizens discussing among themselves and with their elected representatives what they think the government should or should not do, on a host of difficult issues. Ours is a country of vast size and remarkable diversity of opinion. For all of us to live together peacefully and productively, we must embrace the notion that there should be a process of discussion and education before an issue is resolved.

When citizens listen to different viewpoints, they come to understand that politicians typically can't resolve difficult disputes quickly because there is much disagreement in the country about what the tough issues are and how they should be resolved. An exchange of views enables a new understanding: People think beyond their own private interests and are forced to think not just for themselves but for the good of the community and the country. Dialogue demonstrates to citizens that politics is not a bad thing.

There is a magic about democracy. Even when an issue isn't neatly resolved, a healthy dialogue helps us live with disagreement and move on. Whenever I visited those conversations in an Indiana town, I left thinking that the dialogue of democracy, when properly conducted, is the foundation of government of the people.

That system of government established more than two centuries ago is certainly not perfect. It can be difficult to understand, chaotic, slow, and frustrating. Yet I believe it provides the best way for us to deal with our nation's challenges. George Washington's early assessment is still the right one, that "the government, though not absolutely perfect, is one of the best in the world."[5]

It is a commonplace observation to praise the wisdom of the country's founders, but it is also necessary for us to appreciate continually the remarkable system they put together. The representative democracy envisioned by our Constitution has been strong enough to preserve the fragile union, strong enough to promote the general welfare, and strong enough to prevent tyranny.

Virtually all other nations that were in existence in 1787 have had to alter their form of government significantly in the intervening years. Yet the United States, adhering to its original written Constitution, has continued with its form of government essentially unchanged. Ours is one of the oldest nations in the world to have found precisely the government that suits it best.

At the same time, our system can be strengthened as we strive to meet the challenges of this new century. The suggestions I've outlined in this book include

• improving the free and open discussion and mutual education between the representative and represented that lies at the heart of representative democracy;

• better understanding the role of politics and compromise in our system of government, as our way of resolving differences and keeping our nation from coming apart at the seams;

• recognizing the fundamental role Congress plays in our system of government—acting as a balance against a too powerful single leader and preserving the liberty of the American people;

• recognizing the daily impact of the work of Congress—that even if it sometimes gets in the way, it can be enormously helpful to people in their effort to succeed and to live safer, healthier, more secure lives;

• looking at Congress with a balanced eye for both its strengths and weaknesses, and working for specific reforms to improve its operations and make it a more effective and accountable body;

• recognizing the importance of conveying to elected representatives complaints about how Congress operates, which is fundamental to correcting the system and changing course when it gets out of balance;

• strengthening the civic foundations of our country by getting more involved in both the work of Congress and our local communities; and

• restoring in our lives a greater sense of the public good—looking beyond what is good for any one of us, to what is good for the whole country and its future.

All of us should strive for a larger vision, the kind exemplified by Daniel Webster when he said, "Let us develop the resources of our land, call forth its powers, build up its institutions, promote all its great interests, and see whether we also, in our day and generation, may not perform something worthy to be remembered."[6]

As for the future, I do not for a moment agree with those who think that the American system has failed or that the future of the country is bleak. Despite the many challenges facing our nation, we are the world's strongest military power, have the world's largest and most competitive economy, and we are still viewed worldwide as the land of opportunity where people have a chance to become the best they can be. There is a reason why more people seek entry into this nation than any other. Congress, of course, did not single-handedly bring about all these accomplishments, but it played a major role in each of them.

My favorite description of Congress is that we have had many presidents but no kings, and the Congress is principally responsible for that. For more than two centuries Congress has preserved free government and prevented tyranny. It is still the protector of our freedom and the premier forum for addressing the key issues of the day and connecting our voices to the counsels of power. All of us need to look at Congress realistically, critically, even skeptically. But we also need to view it at times with a sense of gratitude and a sense that it has mattered. It not only makes a difference in our lives. It also helps us make a difference in the lives of others.

Our great experiment in representative democracy has served us well, but it fundamentally rests upon informed citizens who understand the essential nature of our system and participate in our civic life. That is how Congress truly works.

Appendix

Communicating with Congress

There are many ways for citizens to communicate with their members of Congress: phone, mail, fax, e-mail, or in person. Here are some sources to help you identify and then connect with your House representative or your senators.

Identifying Your Members of Congress

Find your Senators: http://www.senate.gov
Find your House Representative: http://www.house.gov

Making Contact by Phone

Senate switchboard: 202-224-3121
House switchboard: 202-225-3121

Making Contact by Mail

Write to any member of the Senate at this address:
    The Honorable (full name)
    U.S. Senate
    Washington, DC 20510
Write to any member of the House at this address:
    The Honorable (full name)
    U.S. House of Representatives
    Washington, DC 20515

Making Contact by E-mail

For the Senate: http://www.senate.gov/contacting/index.cfm
For the House: http://www.house.gov/writerep/wyrfaqs.htm#listrep

Making Contact in Person

Members of Congress have offices both in Washington, D.C., and in their state/district. To schedule an appointment or to learn times of local public meetings, call or e-mail.

Communication Tips:

1. State the purpose of your contact clearly. If commenting on a specific piece of legislation, give its bill number.
2. Be brief.
3. Lawmakers understand that people are often upset, but try to be courteous.
4. Use your own words to explain how the issue affects you or your family personally.
5. Be as accurate as possible. Getting your facts straight is essential.
6. Keep in mind that members of Congress really do want to hear your views.

Notes

1. The Role of Congress

1. James Madison, *The Federalist*, no. 51, February 6, 1788.
2. John Adams, included in *The Founders' Constitution*, ed. Philip B. Kurland and Ralph Lerner (Chicago: University of Chicago Press, 1987), chap. 11, document 16.
3. Bernard Bailyn, *To Begin the World Anew* (New York: Alfred A. Knopf, 2003), p. 4.
4. John Adams, included in *The Founders' Constitution*, chap. 4, document 5.
5. Thomas Jefferson, included in *The Founders' Constitution*, chap. 8, document 44.
6. See James Burnham, *Congress and the American Tradition* (Chicago: Henry Regnery, 1959), p. 98.
7. See Walter J. Oleszek, *Congressional Procedures and the Policy Process*, 4th ed. (Washington, D.C.: CQ Press, 1996), p. 19.
8. James Madison, *The Federalist*, no. 58, February 20, 1788.
9. Both quotations from James H. Hutson, *To Make All Laws: The Congress of the United States, 1789–1989* (Boston: Houghton Mifflin, 1990).
10. Richard Henry Lee, included in *The Founders' Constitution*, chap. 14, document 21.
11. Quoted in Louis Brandeis, quoted in *Government by Judiciary: A Transformation of the Fourteenth Amendment*, 2d ed. (Indianapolis: Liberty Fund, 1997), p. 384.
12. Quoted in Val J. Halamandaris, ed., *Heroes of the U.S. Congress: A Search for the Hundred Greatest Members of Congress* (Washington, D.C.: Caring, 1994), p. 193.

2. The Impact of Congress

1. Halamandaris, *Heroes of the U.S. Congress*, p. 143.
2. See Paul Charles Light, *Government's Greatest Achievements: From Civil Rights to Homeland Defense* (Washington, D.C.: Brookings Institution Press, 2002).

3. How Congress Works

1. Artemus Ward, quoted in *Government in America: People, Politics, and Policy*, 9th ed., ed. George C. Edwards III, Martin P. Wattenberg, and Robert L. Lineberry (New York: Longman, 2000), p. 370.

2. Woodrow Wilson, *Congressional Government,* 2d ed. (Boston: Houghton Mifflin, 1885), p. 69.

3. See Alan Rosenthal, Karl T. Kurtz, John Hibbing, and Burdett Loomis, *The Case for Representative Democracy: What Americans Should Know about Their Legislatures* (Denver: National Conference of State Legislatures, 2001), chap. 3.

4. Quoted in Roger H. Davidson and Walter J. Oleszek, *Congress and Its Members,* 6th ed. (Washington, D.C.: Congressional Quarterly, 1998), p. 8.

5. Quoted in Hutson, *To Make All Laws,* p. 5.

6. John Adams to Abigail Adams, October 9, 1774, Massachusetts Historical Society, Adams Family Archive.

4. Public Criticisms of Congress

1. David McCullough, Bicentennial Address to Congress, March 2, 1989.

2. Halamandaris, *Heroes of the U.S. Congress,* p. 98.

3. Rep. John Young Brown of Kentucky, House floor debate, February 4, 1875.

4. Halamandaris, *Heroes of the U.S. Congress,* p. 42.

5. Ibid., p. 26.

6. Bailyn, *To Begin the World Anew,* p. 124.

5. Key Ways Congress Could Work Better

1. See Lee H. Hamilton, with Jordan Tama, *A Creative Tension: The Foreign Policy Roles of the President and Congress* (Washington, D.C.: Woodrow Wilson Center Press, 2002).

2. Wilson, *Congressional Government,* p. 195.

3. Hubert H. Humphrey quoted in David W. Adamany and George E. Agree, *Political Money: A Strategy for Campaign Financing in America* (Baltimore: Johns Hopkins University Press, 1975), p. 8.

4. See Hutson, *To Make All Laws,* p. 25.

5. See John R. Hibbing and Elizabeth Theiss-Morse, *Congress as Public Enemy: Public Attitudes toward American Political Institutions* (New York: Cambridge University Press, 1995), p. 1.

6. Civic Participation

1. Quoted in Thomas E. Patterson, *The American Democracy,* 5th ed. (Boston: McGraw Hill, 2001), p. 184.

2. Quoted in Stephen E. Frantzich, *Citizen Democracy: Political Activists in a Cynical Age* (Lanham, Md.: Rowman and Littlefield, 1999), p. 7.

3. See Michael Schudson, *The Good Citizen: A History of American Civic Life* (Cambridge: Harvard University Press, 1999), p. 311.

4. For these and other examples, see Frantzich, *Citizen Democracy,* and George C. Edwards et al., *Government in America: People, Politics, and Policy.*

5. Quoted in Stanley Elkins and Eric McKitrick, *The Age of Federalism: The Early American Republic, 1788–1800* (New York: Oxford University Press, 1995), p. 75.

6. Halamandaris, *Heroes of the U.S. Congress,* p. 197.

Index

Adams, John, 3, 5, 72, 74, 121–22
Adams, Samuel, 3
Albert, Carl, 41, 61, 64
American Revolution, 4
Antiquities Act (1906), 39

Bailyn, Bernard, 4–5, 89
balance of powers, 2–3, 6–8, 9–10, 145; between Congress and the president, 2, 6–8, 9–11, 103–104, 106–108; Constitutional framework for, 7, 12, 22; and federalism, 11–13; and the founders, 2, 6–8, 11, 12, 21–22, 66–67; and protection of individual liberties/freedom, 2–3, 21–23
Bill of Rights, 7, 21–22, 38
Boggs, Hale, 40
Boggs, Lindy, 41
Bolling, Richard, 40
Brandeis, Louis, 23
Bray, William, 100
Brockovich, Erin, 139
budget, federal: and long-term planning, 113; and powers of Congress, 16–18; and public criticisms of spending, 78–80; reform of budget process, 45–46
Burton, Harold, 40

campaign finance reform, 114–16. *See also* money
Cannon, Joseph, 37, 88
Cellar, Emanuel, 63
civic participation, 124–47; American ambivalence about, 124–25; and campaign work, 131; and congressional elections, 128–29; and the cornerstones of active citizenship, 132–34; discouraging rates of, 126, 127, 128–29; education and being informed, 130, 133; encouraging, 128–31, 146; and individuals who have made a difference, 138–41; and interest groups, 131; the Internet and cyberpolitics, 130; involve-

ment in local issues/communities, 131, 134, 140–41, 146; and media, 131; and mutual communication/dialogue, 95, 125–28, 130, 133, 134–38, 144–45; and party involvement, 131; and political activism, 131; and representative democracy, 124, 126, 127, 130, 132, 144–47; and role of the people in democracy, 141–43; and voting, 128–29, 132–33
Civil Rights Act (1964), 40, 56
Civil War, 15
civility, declining, 47, 98–100
Clay, Henry, 10, 38
Clean Air Act (1970), 34
Clinton, Bill, 6, 27, 59, 104, 113
Clinton, Hillary, 107
committee work: and chairmanships, 65; as congressional duty, 50, 73; ethics committees, 108–10; and open proceedings, 47
common good, 120–22, 146
consensus building and compromise, 52, 62, 86, 87–89, 145
constituent representation, 45, 49–50, 52–55, 90–92, 142–43; and advocacy, 50, 91; and dialogue, 95, 125–28, 133, 134–38, 144–45; frustrations of, 73; methods of, 92; and public criticisms of Congress, 52–53, 54, 90–92; and size of constituencies, 45, 91, 92; and tension between representative and legislative functions, 55; and voting responsibilities of members, 69, 84, 90. *See also* public contact with Congress; public criticisms of Congress
Constitution, U.S.: and balance of powers, 7, 12, 22; Bill of Rights to, 7, 21–22, 38; compromises of, 87–88; and congressional ethics, 109; contemporary Americans' faith in, 8; and federal budget, 16, 18; and foreign policy, 19; Fourteenth Amendment, 56; and House elections, 91; and individual liberties, 21–22; and legislative powers, 14;

Lee H. Hamilton was U.S. Representative from Indiana's Ninth District from 1965 to 1999. He served as Chairman of the House Committee on Foreign Affairs, the Permanent Select Committee on Intelligence, the Joint Economic Committee, and the Joint Committee on the Organization of Congress, and worked to promote the integrity and efficiency of Congress as an institution. He is now Director of the Woodrow Wilson International Center for Scholars in Washington, D.C., and Director of the Center on Congress at Indiana University.